Ruby of Trowutta

Ruby of Trowutta
Recollections of a country postmistress

Collected, compiled and edited by
Christobel Mattingley

With illustrations by
Janet Fenton

Published by
Montpelier Press
PO Box 196
North Hobart Tasmania 7002 Australia

www.montpelierpress.com

Copyright © 2003 Christobel Mattingley

All rights reserved. No part of this publication may be reproduced, stored in a retrieval system, or transmitted in any form or by any means (electronic, mechanical, photocopying, recording, or otherwise), without the prior permission of both the copyright holder and the publisher.

The recording of these tapes was facilitated by a Special Purpose Grant from the Literature Board of the Australia Council in 1982.

The publication of this book was assisted through Arts Tasmania by the Premier, Minister for State Development.

Typesetting and design by Cate Lowry, ACYS Publishing
Set in AlBouwsmaScript, Stone Sans, and Stone Serif 9.5/12.5
Front and back cover photos: Cate Lowry, courtesy of Rosny Historic Centre
Printed by Franklin Press, Hobart

National Library of Australia Cataloguing-in-Publication data:
Mattingley, Christobel, 1931–
Ruby of Trowutta: recollections of a country postmistress
ISBN 1 876597 11 9

1. Paul, Ruby, 1893–1988. 2. Postmasters – Tasmania – Biography.
3. Tasmania – Social conditions – 1851–1901. 4. Tasmania – Social conditions – 1901–1945. I. Title

383.42092

For Madge, Heather, Merle and Lilian

and for all Ruby's descendants

Contents

Dedication		v
The family of Ruby Paul		viii
Timeline		ix
Acknowledgments		x
Discovering a national treasure		xi
Map		xv
Chapter 1	Born in strife	1
2	Childhood home	7
3	Work and play	17
4	The Porteus family	29
5	A wedding to remember	39
6	Scotchtown	45
7	Trowutta	55
8	The top end	63
9	Colin Paul	69
10	The farm	75
11	Building the dunny	87
12	Housekeeping and homemaking	95
13	Balls and bazaars	103
14	Buttermilk and cabbage	113
15	The Post Office	127
16	Emergencies	137
17	The shop	143
18	The butcher shop	153
19	Visitors	163
20	Weddings and christenings	171
21	Remedies and recipes	177
22	Royals and a medal	185
Afterword		189

The family of Ruby Paul

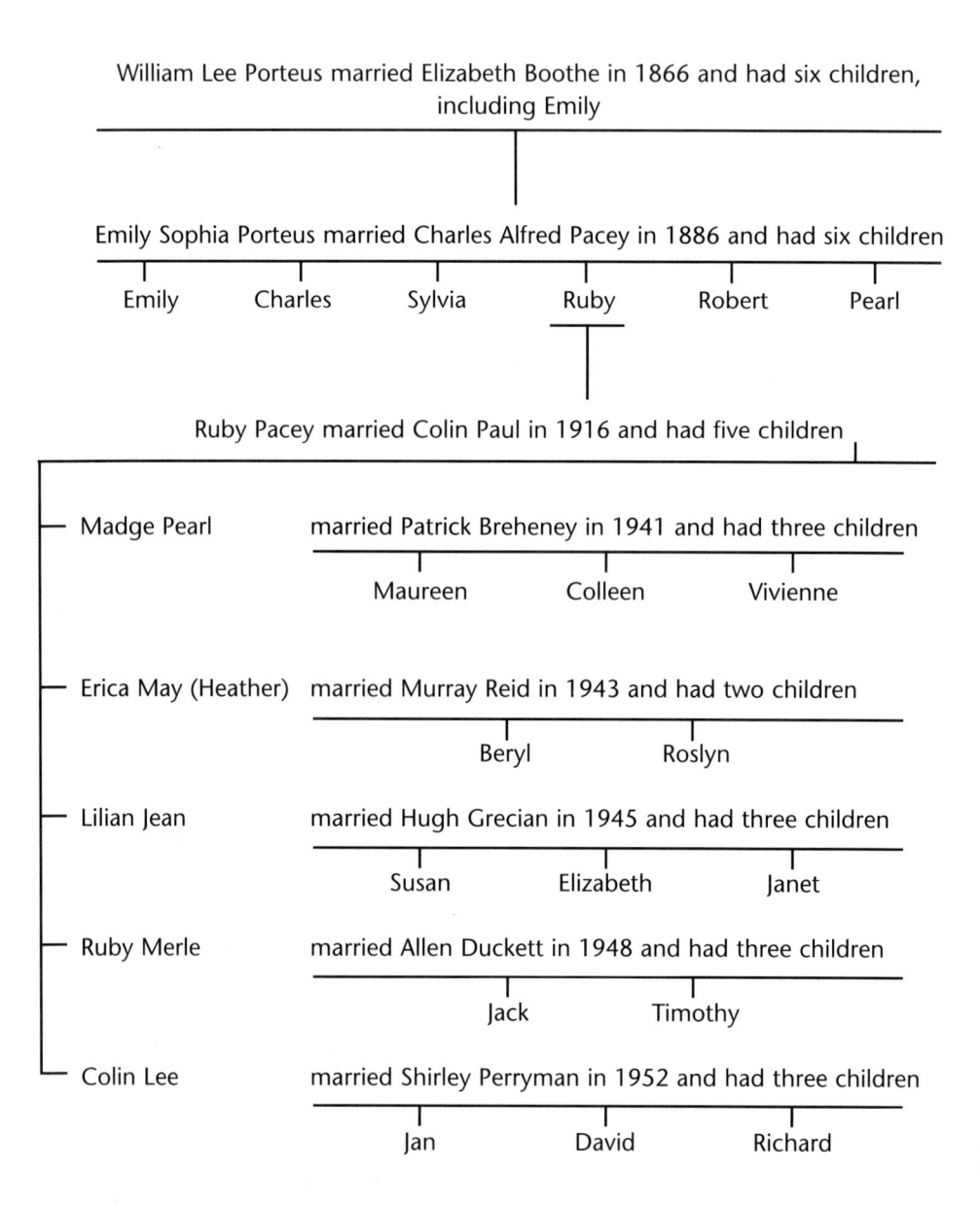

William Lee Porteus married Elizabeth Boothe in 1866 and had six children, including Emily

Emily Sophia Porteus married Charles Alfred Pacey in 1886 and had six children

| Emily | Charles | Sylvia | Ruby | Robert | Pearl |

Ruby Pacey married Colin Paul in 1916 and had five children

- Madge Pearl — married Patrick Breheney in 1941 and had three children
  - Maureen, Colleen, Vivienne

- Erica May (Heather) — married Murray Reid in 1943 and had two children
  - Beryl, Roslyn

- Lilian Jean — married Hugh Grecian in 1945 and had three children
  - Susan, Elizabeth, Janet

- Ruby Merle — married Allen Duckett in 1948 and had three children
  - Jack, Timothy

- Colin Lee — married Shirley Perryman in 1952 and had three children
  - Jan, David, Richard

Timeline

1893	30 December – Ruby Alice Pacey born at Zeehan, Tasmania.
1898	Ruby starts school at Zeehan.
1899	*Outbreak of the Boer War 12 October.* Ruby hears the news at Queenstown while on a coach travelling to Gormanston.
1905	*First selectors take up land on Trowutta Tableland. A hollow tree serves as the first 'post office' and message centre.*
1906	Ruby leaves school, aged 13, works as a mother's help.
1908	Ruby leaves Zeehan, goes to help sister Phyllis at Moina.
ca 1908	Ruby's father, Charles Alfred Pacey, moves to Scotchtown, attempting to make a farm.
ca 1910	Ruby's mother refuses to live at Scotchtown.
1912	Ruby's sister Syl comes to Trowutta as a bride, joining five other married women in the district. *Trowutta Post Office established by Mrs Frost, future mother-in-law of Ruby's sister Pearl, with a weekly mail contract.*
ca 1913	Ruby's mother moves to Trowutta. Ruby's father contracted to make road between Scotchtown and Irishtown.
1914	*World War 1 begins 4 August.* Ruby moves to Scotchtown, works as a housekeeper, meets her future husband, Colin Paul.
1915	William and Eliza Porteus, Ruby's grandparents, come from Strahan to live at Trowutta. Ruby's father dies at Scotchtown in June. *First sod turned at Irishtown for the railway to Trowutta. First school opens at Trowutta.*
1916	Ruby marries Colin Paul on Porteus grandparents' Golden Wedding anniversary, 22 March. Colin and Ruby build their first house at Mopoke Gully on Trowutta Hill (also known as Cuckoo Hill).
1917	Ruby's first child, Madge, born, 11 January.
1919	Ruby's second child, Heather, born, 30 January. *Opening of Stanley-Trowutta railway line, 2 July. This led to the establishment of many timber mills in the district.*
1920	Colin and Ruby move to Roger River to live in 'The Red House'.
1921	Ruby's third child, Lilian, born 30 April. *First picture show at Trowutta in new hall.*
1922	Paul family moves back to 'Nesdale', a farm at the top end of Trowutta.
1923	Ruby's fourth child, Merle, born 12 April. *First cars at Trowutta.*
1928	Ruby's fifth child, Colin, born 22 June.
1930	The Pauls take over Trowutta Post Office and shop 1 May.
1939	*World War Two begins 3 September.*
1940	Ruby's husband Colin dies 6 May.
1947	Ruby appointed a Justice of the Peace for the district of Circular Head.
1950	Ruby's mother dies in Melbourne.
1951	*Electricity connected to Trowutta.*
1971	Ruby leaves the Post Office because of ill health.
1972	Ruby invested with Imperial Service Medal 20 October.
1988	January – Ruby dies in her 95th year.

Conversion table

1 mile = 1.61 km
1 yard = 0.914 m
1 foot = 30.5 cm
1 inch = 25.4 mm
1 pound (lb) = 454 g
1 ounce (oz) = 28.3 g
1 gallon (gal) = 4.55 litres
1 pint = 568 mL

Study notes

Teachers' study notes are available from www.montpelierpress.com

Acknowledgements

As well as all the help, hospitality and interest from Ruby's daughters Heather, Madge, Merle and Lilian, I would like to thank Alison Smith, also of the Porteus clan, compiler of the Porteus family tree, whose assistance with photographs has been most generous. Rhonda Hamilton of the Queen Victoria Museum, Launceston, was helpful in copying old family photos. Chris Pearce of the Hobart Bookshop, whose wife Janet is one of Ruby's granddaughters, has always encouraged the project, as have Janet Fenton, whose illustrations enhance the text, Debbie McGowan, Beth Miller, and Stephanie Rhodes, all of Penguin Books. I am grateful to Christine Howard who urged me to entrust the ms to Montpelier Press, to Elizabeth Dean, the Montpelier editor who responded so positively to Ruby's story, to Sheila Allison, the editor who took it on at short notice after Elizabeth Dean's untimely death, and to Cate Lowry for her attention to design and production details.

I acknowledge research assistance from the State Library of Tasmania on several queries, and a grant from Arts Tasmania to support publication.

Christobel Mattingley

I would like to thank those who assisted me with research for the images in this book: Annie Ward, Channel Historical and Folk Museum Association Inc.; Elspeth Wishart, Tasmanian Museum and Art Gallery; Louise James, Queen Victoria Museum and Art Gallery; Huon Valley Apple and Heritage Museum; Tasmaniana Library; State Reference Service, State Library of Tasmania; The Sound Preservation Association of Tasmania Inc.; Narryna Heritage Museum; Rosny Historic Centre; Geoff Fenton and Madge Breheney.

Janet Fenton

Discovering a national treasure

I was privileged to meet Ruby Paul and her family in January 1975 through her daughter Heather Reid and have valued their friendship ever since. When Heather learned of my interest in the Mount Lyell settlements on Tasmania's West Coast, she offered to introduce me to her mother, who had been born in the nearby mining town of Zeehan and spent time as a girl with relatives at Gormanston, a Lyell township.

Ruby, a spry eighty-two, made us wonderfully welcome and cooked and served a splendid meal in her charming little Smithton home. Primed with copious cups of tea, she began to tell of her early childhood at Zeehan, then in its heyday as one of the world's most important silver-lead fields. Her memories were crystal clear, her words vivid and vibrant, she was warm with a lifetime of living, loving and laughing. I was captivated and knew I had discovered a national treasure. Unfortunately, but understandably, she was tape-recorder shy. So I sat and scribbled down her words until she declared it was time for cups of tea again.

Her story had such integrity and identity that I was unwilling to use any of it for my own purposes. I suggested then and there that it should be told, but Ruby was totally unassuming and saw nothing special about her life and her achievements.

Over the years my husband and I visited her a number of times and I got to know all the members of her family. When she was well into her eighties she accompanied Heather and me on one of our trips to the West Coast, revisiting scenes of her childhood at Zeehan, Strahan, Gormanston and Queenstown. On the site of the Zeehan house we even found a piece of fluted glass, amethyst with age, which Ruby recognised as part of her mother's sugar bowl.

In 1983 I wrote asking once again, at the risk of spoiling a beautiful friendship, if she would allow me to tape her. Fortunately I had followed up our first meeting in 1975 with a visit to her sisters Syl and Pearl and brother Charl in Melbourne. I had particularly hoped to gain from her brother some information I was seeking. But although they were all willing to be taped, they did not have the clarity of memory and recall which was Ruby's outstanding gift. Charl died not long afterwards and a couple of years later I sent Ruby a copy of the recording I had made. Although at first the family were reluctant to listen to it, when they eventually did, they were thrilled.

With all its family banter, clatter of teacups, ringing of doorbells and interruptions by neighbours, it was a transcriber's nightmare, but a delight and relief to Ruby and her daughters, who had perhaps feared that recording might be more formal and clinical. So finally, persuaded by her daughters, Ruby agreed to be taped.

In October 1983 I spent a memorable week staying first at Ruby's in Smithton, where daughters Madge Breheney and Merle Duckett joined in the fun, priming the pump of their mother's amazing memory. Then we went back to Heather's home in Devonport, where the old black kettle was always steaming on the hob for the many cups of tea which carried us on far into the nights of nostalgia, and where Ruby demonstrated how to make her renowned potato cake, cut into farrels.

We also made a sentimental journey back to Trowutta, where the old Pacey home was then still standing under towering cypress pines and tiny-flowered fuchsias brought as slips long ago from an Irish hedgerow, which had since grown branches as thick as a man's arm. We wandered through the silent empty rooms which had resounded to the crowd assembled for Ruby's wedding when the house was barely finished.

We paused in the kitchen, 'a cosy room with a roaring fire', cold now and the old tin chimney outside leaning ominously. Here Gran Porteus had sat in her black dress, Bible on knee with penny romance tucked inside, smacking her lips over her favourite buttermilk, waited on by her daughter, Emily Sophia Pacey, Ruby's mother, from daybreak to starlight.

We walked along the verandah where Grandfather Porteus had cherished his tobacco plants in pots, and into the yard, now engulfed in blackberries, where he had hidden his bottle of whisky under the sprouting potatoes in the shed. In the front garden daffodils and snowdrops were flowering, japonica was red with blossom, and Gran Pacey's holly bush still looked good for many Christmases to come.

We visited the site of the 'Post Office tree' and Ruby's first married home on Cuckoo Hill, and had a picnic at the Showground, where reputations had been made or lost over the height of a sponge cake or the combination of flowers in an arrangement.

We retraced the route from the school, now gone, sold to become a piggery at Edith Creek, and where the trees Heather planted with pride as a child have been cut down. We crossed Spinks Creek now overgrown with blackberries, where Madge caught the lobster, drove past Cossie Corner, where cosmos are no longer to be seen; then up the road where it was common to see a dozen snake tracks in the white dust on a summer afternoon; on up to Nesdale, the Paul family's third house at the top end, before they moved to the Post Office.

Back to the Post Office and shop, now displaying signs for Coca Cola and Peters icecream, and the old weatherboard house to which they were joined, with its front room where the dentist pulled teeth and the garden where he threw them afterwards. All altered now, almost beyond recognition.

The local hall, venue for dances, pictures and all sorts of district celebrations, has been converted to a house. At Edith Creek, the Area School – on land given by a member of the Porteus family – became the venue for the first family reunion in 1989 and brought together over 300 Porteus descendants from all across Australia.

In 1983 remnants of the great myrtle forests which had covered the plateau could still be seen along the roads – piles of gigantic logs pushed against boundaries to form fences. In 1991 even they were gone, replaced by barbed wire. And the robins, wrens and 'dukewillies' were long gone too, their places taken by pigeons, sparrows and starlings in great flocks, feeding on the pastures which have replaced the forests.

In those seven days in October 1983, Ruby, only two months short of her ninetieth birthday, and her daughters Madge, Heather and Merle filled eighteen 90-minute tapes with memories spanning ninety years, memories of life rich not in a material sense, but in spirit. It was practical, down to earth, day by day living, doing what had to be done, with energy, humour and perseverance – whether it was delivering milk or a baby, feeding the family, building a dunny or contriving fancy dress for a ball – giving generously of time, talent and whatever else they had to help their neighbours or anyone in need.

As postmistress and storekeeper, Ruby was the lynchpin of the Trowutta district for over forty years. Through their memories, shared with such vivacity and in such authentic detail, she and her daughters have recreated a picture of a way of life which was common, almost universal in country districts and which has now all but disappeared. Their memories celebrate the closeness of community in an isolated area, a sense and spirit of community now changed by modern transport and communications and the expectations of a consumer society.

Totally unselfconsciously, Ruby and her daughters revealed themselves, their actions, attitudes and values, giving a generous 'slice of life', invaluable as a page of social history. With humour and without sentiment, yet with sensitivity, they brought to life through their rich store of anecdotes the people with whom their lives were so closely intertwined.

Heather, who was not sent away like her siblings for further education but kept at home to help during the Great Depression, has made the biggest contribution to the Trowutta section of these memoirs. I am especially grateful to her for facilitating my collecting of the story, and working painstakingly with me through all the tapes, transcripts and drafts. I am also grateful to the other daughters, Madge, Merle and Lilian, for their support.

The memories of Ruby and her family evoke an era and its values; a community and its spirit; a family, its kinship, loyalties and faith in its members through four generations, and its celebration of its Irish heritage.

CM

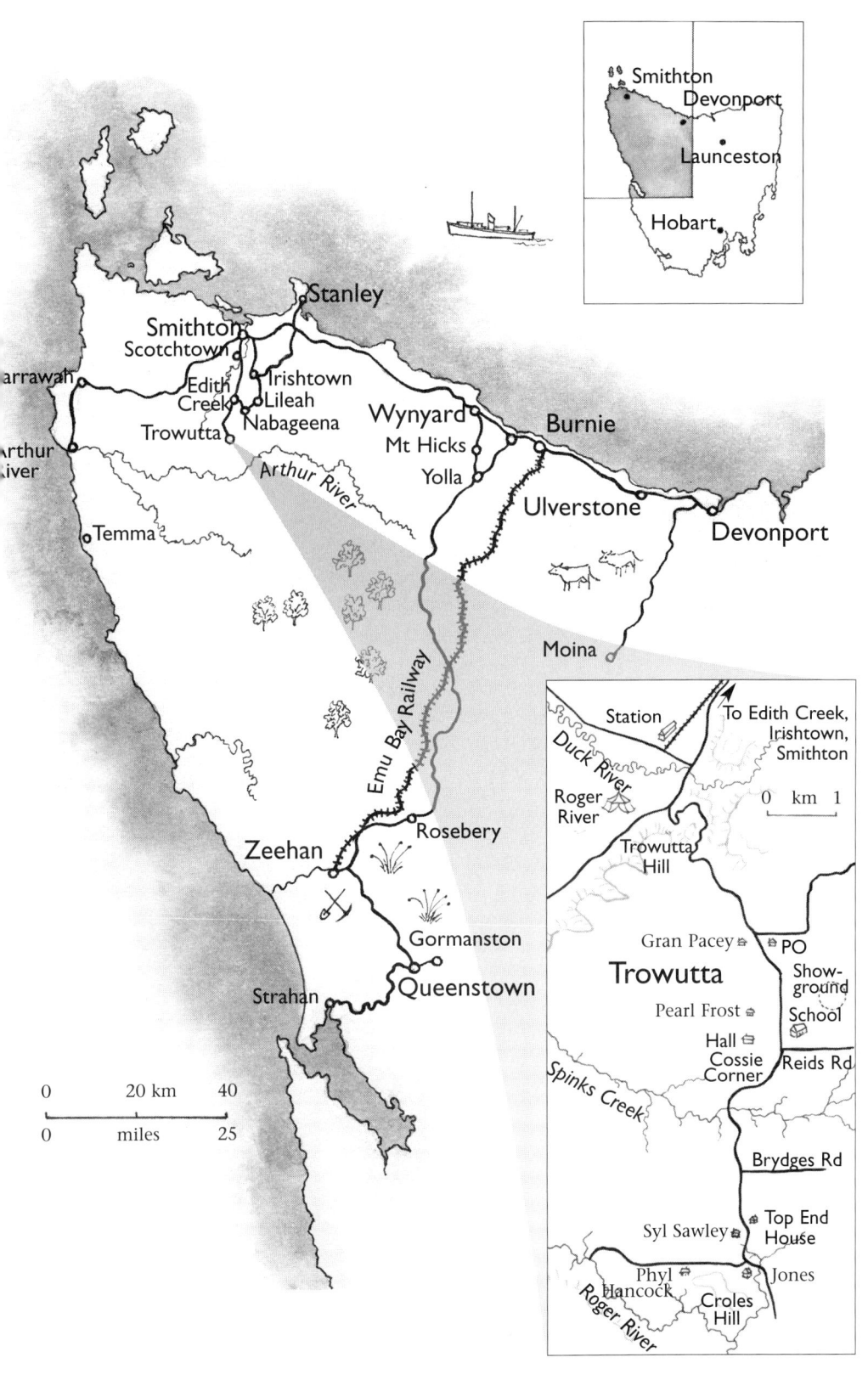

Ruby Paul, about 1940

Chapter 1

Born in strife

> "Mother gave the old woman a good kick and out popped the baby! Me!"

Ruby Alice Paul (nee Pacey) was born on 30 December 1893 at Zeehan, a boom town on the rich silver-lead mining fields of Tasmania's rugged West Coast. The Pacey family had just that year arrived from Hobart, the capital, by sea. It was a voyage to be dreaded around the wild South West Cape and up the stormy west coast to Strahan, and Emily Sophia Pacey (nee Porteus) was probably already pregnant with her fourth child.

Strahan, situated on Macquarie Harbour, was port for the mining fields at both Zeehan and Queenstown. The harbour, notorious for its penal settlement in the colony's early days, had to be entered across a bar, appropriately named Hell's Gates, scene of many a shipwreck.

At Zeehan, thirty miles inland, where mines with romantic names like Silver Queen and Silver King had started barely three years before, conditions were rough and amenities were minimal. But Ruby's mother, well-born and gently reared in Ireland, met the challenges with spirit.

Ruby remembers

The family had all just come from Hobart. Phyl and Syl and Charl all had the measles and they were in a hut on one side of the road, and Auntie Minnie, Mother's sister, was looking after them. There was a big picnic in Moss Park over the river, and they got out in their nighties and watched the sports, while Mother was having this baby in another hut.

She must have always had very hard births. She'd never tell you, but I just heard different things dropped here and there. There was an old woman named Mrs White with her, and she had a big dog called Leo. I suppose Mother was lucky to get anyone. She was very very bad and the old woman got very frightened. She shut the door on Mother and went away calling, 'Leo, Leo, come on, Leo'. Mother said she could hear her getting further away, leaving her there by herself.

The old woman went to a Mrs Dudley, who lived a fair way away, and said, 'It's shelfed, Mistress. I can't get that baby. That woman's very bad'.

Mrs Dudley said, 'And have you come over here and left her by herself?' She took the poker, a great big iron poker, and she chased her all the way back.

Mother was shut in this hut by herself. The baby was still shelfed and Mother said to herself, 'Well,' she said, 'I'm dying anyway and nobody can help me'. So when the old woman came in the door she thought, 'I'm going to die anyway, so I'll give her a good kick'.

So she gave her a good kick and out popped the baby! Me! So I was born in strife, wasn't I? That's the truth.

Mother and Aunt Minnie both got to hate the sight of this old woman because she didn't, just wouldn't, do much herself. Perhaps she used to like a drop of whisky. They used to sew binders on the babies then. And she'd say, 'Where's me needles, Mistress?, Where's me needles?' So Auntie Minnie used to say, 'Go to the Devil and find them!'

All babies had binders, a strip of flannel about a couple of inches wide. That was tied tight and then if the navel wasn't quite good they used to put a coin on it and bind it over again. Mother used to bring a lot of babies into the world and she used to get a bit of real linen, and she'd hold it in front of the fire until it was scorched to sterilise it and put that round the navel, when it was tied and fixed up. Over the top of the flannel binder they had a canvas binder, real heavy canvas. You'd only have one that would do all your family and then you'd give it to somebody else. They used to bind that real tight on the baby.

Then they had 'the long flannel'. It was a strip of flannel with a little piece cut out for under the arms, all bound round. It had a hole and two tapes to thread through. You'd fold that over and that would tie round the baby. It had a full skirt all gathered in and you'd fold that over the baby's feet. Then there was a calico gown over the top. That was all they wore.

Babies were kept in the 'long flannel' till they were six weeks old, then they were short-coated. You made three of these nice little gowns. They had lovely little yokes and torchon lace, and some were embroidered around the bottom. I mostly had embroidery round the neck for my babies and torchon lace all down the yoke. The yoke was double, pin-tucked by hand. Then you had little dresses. Little boys wore dresses until they were about two or three, mostly made of red turkey twill. Mother hated red turkey twill and she'd never buy it. She always had something else.

I always wanted a red dress. I got one when I was about ten or twelve. It was red with a little white curly pattern in it and I thought it was lovely. Mother didn't buy it. It was Phyllis, my oldest sister, that bought the material. She was learning dressmaking at the time. I wore it when I went to stay with my Auntie Bella at Gormanston and when I was helping my Uncle Peter tar the roof I got a big blob of tar all down one side. I wore it to school long afterwards.

The first machine we had was at Zeehan. Father thought he'd make a big fellow of himself and put a deposit on a machine for Phyllis. It was a Singer and it was fourteen pounds. Mother never got that much, and she then had to pay for it, half a crown a week out of the housekeeping. It's a really beautiful sewing machine and Phyllis's daughter still makes all her clothes on it and it runs as smooth as anything. Well, that's what I learned to sew on. I was ten and it was a wet Boxing Day. We were going to the beach and it was too wet, so Mother let me sew on the machine. From then on I made all the family's underclothes. The material was always white, finer than calico, nainsook they called it. Winceyette was a cotton wincey. Real wincey was a very fine Scottish material with a nap.

My cousin Myrtle, Auntie Minnie's daughter, started school the day I did. I'd never let her get ahead of me and she was a year and three months older and rather clever, very studious. We went to school together and on the first day we were too shy to go out when the other kids went out, and we sat with our elbows on the desk. The teacher came and she brought us both a cup of cocoa. We had a lovely teacher, Miss Fleming, and her sister was a teacher too. She was a bit older and as crabby as the dickens.

One day they put me up [a class] and they didn't put Myrtle up, so she cried and they had to put her up. I think they must have got us mixed because she was doing better work than me. But I was always proud because I beat her for once. I was always the youngest girl in the class and I was a duffer.

We always went to school together and we'd come home together. She came from a different direction and we'd meet at The Bonnet Box, a drapery store. Mother and Auntie used to meet there too, always at a certain time. Myrtle and I had a new velvet cap each, a little round velvet cap with a tassel over the back. Myrtle was nearly like a twin sister to me. We just did everything together and we used to tell each other every mortal thing. We used to go and sit in the dunny to watch the bees when we had to watch for them swarming. And she told me every book she ever read. She'd tell me the story and I'd tell her what I'd read.

I wasn't six when I started school. I left when I was thirteen and then I had to go back for six weeks at the end of the year because it came in that we had to go to school until we were fourteen. I'd been looking after women having babies. And I had to go back to school!

They were good schools at Zeehan and we did learn. There were two big state schools, a great big convent school and a private school. About 300 or more went to our school. And there was another big state school at the top end of Zeehan.

Our school had three very big rooms. One room had the lower first and the upper first. We used to say 'The ABC'. They were all the little ones. The second and third classes were in another room, one class at one end and the other at the far end. Then there was the fourth, fifth and sixth in another room. The big long desks would hold five. We had slates in the first classes and then we had inkwells and pens with nibs. The headmaster used to teach the fifth and sixth classes, and there was a teacher for the fourth class, a teacher for the second, and another two perhaps.

We had one lesson a week in our reading book and at the top there'd be all the hard words. And at the bottom there'd be so many Latin roots. And we had a week to learn all that and some of the words were so big, so hard for children. There was a poem with a lot of these words we were supposed to know – 'Bullying, bantering, browbeating, ridiculing and maltreating ...' and I suppose then I'd be ten.

You didn't look forward to school then like kiddies do now. We never had school trips or anything like that. I wanted to stay away for a day and always would if I could. If I got a bad cold, I'd be 'Mum, my throat's bad'. And Mother would get a piece of flannel, double it and put eucalyptus on it and she'd put it around my throat. And then she'd tear it in strips and put a smaller strip on each day till I got better. I had some dreadful throats.

Born in strife

Mother kept four cows and we took milk to deliver on our way to school. We each had our own customers and it was a long way out of our way. It was quite a business really. We carried the milk in big tin billies and served three measures, half-pint, pint and a quart. The measure had a hook handle and used to hang inside the can. You'd make a dent in the rim of the can so that the measure would fit in. The lid would be over the top. There were big corridors at school with wide doors and we used to put our milk cans right in behind the door. They were never interfered with.

A lot of us used to walk to school. We always took our lunch – a blackcurrant jam sandwich or bread and butter with pepper. There was always plenty of butter and jam and very nice cheese. It was a good long walk and we used to get into mischief. Sometimes the rivers would be flooded, Pea Soup Creek and the Little Henty. Mother would come to meet us, just to see if we could get home. Often we couldn't go to school, if she thought the river was unsafe. We kids used to live in the Little Henty, collecting wood.

In the winter we used to get very sore legs. It was a sort of frostbite. We all wore long stockings and our legs would get so sore that we couldn't wear our garters. Mother would sew a tape to the stocking tops so we could button it and hold them up on our stays. The stays would be two or three folds of cloth stitched together, fitting round you, very firm. And they'd have buttons to hold your pants, three on the front and three on the back. Your pants were these trapdoor pants. You'd let them down at the back. Every pair of pants you made had six buttonholes. There was quite a lot of making.

We got terrible chilblains too in winter. If we were very troubled Mother would put a tin of water on the stove and before we went to bed we would sit with our feet in this hot water for half an hour. We'd keep adding to it so that it would be as hot as we could bear it, and that would give you a night's sleep. Sometimes your chilblains would get broken, like big broken sores. Then you just didn't know what to do with them. You just had to put up with them.

My father had started a brickworks with a partner – Cassell & Pacey – up the hill by the pinetree on the Dundas road. You can still find bricks with their mark if you go fossicking about where Dundas used to be. The brickyard went broke when the Van Diemen's Land Bank went broke in 1893 and Mr Cassell drowned in the Florence Mine.

Father wouldn't work *for* a boss. He had to *be* the boss. So he went contracting in the mines over at Queenstown and was often away for months. We were very poor then. It wasn't him who suffered. It was us. He'd work very hard, then pay it all out to his men. We didn't have much money. So Mother used to go out of a night nursing.

There was an outbreak of scarlet fever and diphtheria. Kids were dying all over Zeehan. There was a hospital but they weren't ever taken there. Mother would go and sit up most of the night with them. She'd come home early in the morning and Syl would have a tin of water on the chimney. Mother used to go into the shed – it was an open shed, and she'd take off every stitch, and have a bath in hot water before she came in to get us kids up to go to school.

And we took this three drops of turpentine on sugar, but you could taste it all the time. I can still taste it yet. It was awful. A little girl died on each side of us but we never got either scarlet fever or diphtheria, even though Mother used to lay out the bodies. They used to put pennies on their eyelids. There was a photo taken of a boy after he died. His mother hung it over the mantelpiece and used to talk to it. Our cousins got scarlet fever and they were very ill. Mother used to go up there and she'd have a bath when she got home. She'd never come into the house with anything she'd had on. And we were the only ones on the road that didn't get ill.

The doctor would never come to patients unless Mother sent for him. He lived away up the top end of Zeehan right beside the Gaiety Theatre and he had to walk. It was a long way out to our end of town. If they went for him, he'd always say, 'Did Mrs Pacey send for me?' If Mother said to come, he'd come.

Chapter 2

Childhood home

"No children were happier than we were growing up."

Ruby recalls her early home and life at Zeehan in loving and lively detail.

When the family first came to Zeehan they lived in the Railway Hotel, the first one built where they thought the township would be. Well, the township went the other way so this hotel was closed. Then three families lived in it. In the kitchen there was a great big range easily six foot wide and an oven on each side as wide as a door. They never used that stove much. It took too much wood, so Mother always cooked in the camp oven.

Then we went out to live in the place on the Dundas road out of Zeehan over Pea Soup Creek and the Little Henty River. It was only two rooms, the place where I was born. Grandfather came up from Strahan and built a room on at the front. Later one of my brothers fixed a bough roof from the pole at the corner for a verandah. It was a big kitchen and living room Grandfather built us, and he made a little passage where Mother made a pantry. There were two steps up to the bedrooms, where we used to sit.

Everybody had a couch. We had a couch that my father made out of split wood. It had a square seat that could hold four or five. One of my brothers slept on it for years. Mother padded the arms and back somehow, and made cushions. When the couch got shabby every two years or so Mother would cover it with new cretonne. It had a cretonne drape all round with frills at the front and the boots were all kept underneath – except when Pearl wore hers to bed! She was very little and she'd just got her first pair of button-up boots. It was such a treat she went to bed in them. There's these button-up boots coming over the side of the cot and we were all starting to laugh. She was that indignant!

People used to have fenders with lacy wrought iron and a set of fire irons. But we had a wooden fender my father made. It went round the three sides of the hearth. We used to sit on it of a morning by the open fire to put our boots on, even when we were small. We'd always go and sit on the fender. It was just a place where it was always warm and friendly.

We had a great big deal pine table in the middle of the kitchen, scrubbed white. When you finished your meal and tidied the kitchen, we always put a cloth on it and a vase of flowers in the middle and it became the sitting room. Mother bought floral material by the yard and scalloped the edges to make the cloth. Plush or chenille covers were very smart. Later when the family had some money, we had a tapestry cover. When we first went there, it was kitchen/everything.

There was a form of two-inch thick pine the length of the table, at least five foot long, and the children sat on it for meals. Form, chairs and wooden fender were put outside every Saturday for scrubbing. Auntie Minnie scrubbed hers with ashes and her furniture was always as white as snow. But Mother could never get the big brown stain out of one end of our form where our brother Charl had spilt hot bird lime on it. Sandsoap was a great invention.

We never had much to polish, just the brass taps and door knobs, and the brass candlesticks from Ireland. The windows were washed and polished, but they were mostly small panes. We cleaned the lamp chimneys too on Saturdays, while the cakes were cooking. We never had two and six to buy a broom so we went out into the bush and cut teatree for a broom. But no children were happier than we were growing up.

We had a few chairs – just ordinary chairs, Austrian bentwood. The seats would wear out and you would buy new. The ones we had were like plaited cane. We made many a chair. A box turned upside down would be the seat. You used to get beautiful timber in the boxes, and we'd make a cushion for the seat, and put two pieces of wood up for arms and a couple for the back so it would be sloped, and boards

Childhood home

across that. Then we'd pad and cover it with cretonne. Most people had a chair that would be the mother's, which would have no arms. Father's chair would be bigger and have arms. Mother's chair would just have a padded back, so that she could nurse, change and feed the baby. We thought it was a great thing when Mother bought herself a rocking chair. It was imported. Zeehan had wonderful shops then.

gooseberry

We had a big white scrubbed pine dresser and a cupboard – we used to call it a safe – that had perforated zinc sides. That's where you'd keep your meat. The dresser had a cupboard underneath too, three white pine butter boxes which Father fitted with hinged lids. They were for flour, sugar and bread. There were two or three big crocks with pickled onions, jam, and gooseberry chutney. That would be all the furniture.

Mother cooked in a camp oven first. It was always round. Then she got a Peters oven which was square, with a stove hole, made of cast iron. It would take six loaves. It was set up on bricks with a space underneath for a fire, and fire on top. The oven was built into the fireplace with upright pieces welded at the sides and a bar at the front. There were two cranes built into the chimney with pot hooks hanging from chains, to adjust over the fire. Mother would put the lid on the fire to make it hot before putting scones in, then she'd replace the lid and put coals over the top. She made gingerbread too, almost like a short ginger scone. She'd warm treacle and dripping in a saucepan, pat the dough out and cut it with a knife. We'd eat it hot like a tea cake. There'd seldom be any left for next day!

Mother could make interesting food out of simple stuff. What she made was very plain but she'd never skimp. She had her own recipes, but there were ingredients we'd never heard of. I never heard of vanilla until I was nearly grown up. We always had essence of lemon. Jellies were in a hard cube, and when she was making them she'd always give us a little piece.

Emu Bay Railway

Ruby of Trowutta

We usually had a meat meal every day – lots of stews. The camp oven was beautiful for cooking meat, but you couldn't put coals on the lid, because you needed to turn the meat. The meat came in on the Emu Bay Railway from Burnie. You could get any sort of meat. It wasn't very dear. A shin of beef cost a shilling. The butcher would deliver in a basket, but we usually went to the shop.

The baker came every day by horse, with a basket over his arm. It was the most beautiful bread you ever tasted, white and wholemeal, twisted and round cobs, and plain bread cooked without a tin with beautiful crust 'flies'. There were high tin loaves too and pipe loaves. And beautiful buns! They were a special treat. A day-old bun was a ha'penny.

Mother often made Irish potato cake in the camp oven. It was savoury, a complete meal in itself. We wouldn't have anything else but tea. She'd boil a pot of peeled old potatoes with salt, strain them very dry and mash them very well, with no lumps. She had a masher made by Uncle Peter Cameron, of Huon pine, turned on a lathe, shaped like a bottle, three inches diameter at the bottom and a knob at the top. She'd turn the potato out onto the big scrubbed table and work in as much flour as she could and add more salt if needed. She used to take a pinch off the side to taste it. When it was quite pliable with no cracks in it, she'd mould it into a three-cornered point. She'd flatten it with her hand into a circle about the size of a dinner plate, then cut it into 'farrels', like shortbread. She'd cook it in a greased camp oven hung over the fire, turning each farrel. If she was short of dripping she'd just cook it with flour, but it was much nicer with dripping. We loved it.

Our china was blue. There'd be three meat dishes with a set and two vegetable dishes, a big soup tureen and a dozen of everything, every size. Three or four sizes in plates – dinner plates, a bread and butter plate, sometimes a big dinner plate and what they called a dessert plate. But there were no pudding bowls in those days. Even when soup plates first came out they were nearly as big as a dinner plate and they'd have the wide flange.

You very seldom got a set with cups and saucers. You bought cups and saucers separately and for people who could afford them, there were beautiful china tea sets. For ordinary cups, one sort was white with a raised blue daisy. They were beautiful. Most ordinary cups were white with a shamrock in the bottom and a couple of gold lines

camp oven

around the top, in different grades of china. You could get the ordinary thick cups and the very fine china. They were lovely.

We had a little bit of silver, but most of it was only silver plated. We had to clean the knives for a long time. I didn't hear about stainless steel knives until about 1928 or 1929, when my sister Phyl went to Melbourne and she said, 'There's some stainless steel knives!' But the others you could rub up and they'd be sharp. It's a job to get them now. Everybody snaps them up because you can still sharpen them. But some of them are worn now.

We had two brass candlesticks, big twirly ones about fifteen inches high, one at each end of the mantelpiece. They were a bit battered, a bit bent. But we used to have to polish them up. In the middle we had a vase of green reeds that would last from one year to the next. And we used to make artificial flowers to put in it. We'd get pretty sweet papers – silver, gold, red and blue, and we'd get a spray of oats or grass in seed and wrap them around the seed heads and hang them on the reed stalks. And we'd get crepe paper and cut it in strips about two inches wide, pleat it and wind it round and round a stem of button grass, and you'd pull the paper a bit at the edge so that it scalloped. And if you were lucky you put a little bit of green around it and you had a poppy. The button grass knob in the middle was the centre of the poppy.

There were some good pictures on the wall. We used not to get Christmas cards or anything like that then. I don't remember anything about Christmas cards when I was little. But we used to paper the walls every Christmas. Paper was sixpence a roll and we made the paste out of flour and water. The papers had floral patterns. One year Mother chose blue, another time it was autumn tones. There were six of us children and we were let play Blind Man's Buff and games like that, so the paper was always torn by Christmas.

Once our mother saw this passage lino with a pattern so high and she bought enough to make a dado to go round the room. That made the paper last two years. Lots of people did that. You nailed it to the walls – they were usually hand-split palings – and put the scrim and paper above. In some houses the walls were just scrim and paper to the ground and perhaps they'd add a dado later over the top. The scrim was tacked to the palings and the paper was pasted to the scrim.

Some people didn't even have wallpaper. They'd use newspaper or brown paper. But mostly they'd have wallpaper. And the most ghastly stuff it was, if you think of it now. And all round the top where the scrim and paper was, they used to put a little border to match the colours. It was nearly always floral – a frieze. Mother brought that lino to Trowutta.

It was a greeny-grey. We had board floors for a start and then there was lino. We'd perhaps get enough lino for one room at a time.

Everybody had a valance on their mantelpiece. Some were very ornate. Auntie Minnie's had long glass beads in a diamond pattern and it hung down about a foot. It was put round the mantelpiece with fancy headed tacks. They were long flat beads, some green and some silver. We kids thought it was a beautiful thing and I can remember it was worn away in threads because we kids would always want to touch it. Mother used to make hers out of frilled cretonne. When it got smoked and worn out, she'd get another piece.

We only had very ordinary curtains, white lace curtains, but they used to look lovely when they were new. They looked very elegant, washed, starched and ironed. There were no great big windows, just ordinary windows. That was in the early days. I remember buying curtains for half a crown a pair, but they were very cheap ones. You'd pay about five or six shillings for a better pair of curtains and they'd last a couple of years. The cheap ones never looked the same. They'd stretch at the edges and they wouldn't hang so nice after they were washed.

Mother had an iron bed. Some of them were trimmed with brass and sometimes they had white coloured rings and knobs and stainless steel. The good ones would be fairly heavy. They used to be all put together with little screws which would eventually fall out. Where there was a screw there was usually a little bright knob instead of a nut, and kids would screw them off.

We children used to sleep three to a double bed. It was an iron bed with a lattice of metal strips. We had two straw-filled palliasses, which had to be put out to air. There was a canvas cover laced to them, topped with a kapok tick. I can remember the first kapok I saw. You'd buy so many pound. Five pound would make a good single bed. That's when it was new, and then you'd have to put in a bit more after it had settled down. There was one feather and kapok bolster for three children, and good quality white blankets. Mother had the Irish tick, a great big feather tick, pure goose down in a handwoven linen cover, brought out from Ireland.

We made a lot of furniture out of boxes. You'd buy them from the storekeepers. They were heavy pine, but rough. A big square one about four feet high was my mother's dressing table for years. She put shelves in it and made a cover of white hailstone muslin, real full, and then she had this big piece of crochet on top, and that was a dressing table.

We had a bath on Saturday nights in a big tin tub in front of the fire, one child after another. We all washed our faces first and we never washed our hair in the bath. Mother heated the water in four-gallon kerosene tins hung on cranes over the fire. The water had to be carried from the river. We had a couple of wooden casks for water, but no tank.

The toilet was ever so far up the paddock. It was a can which Mother had to empty herself. There was a night cart in the town, but he didn't come as far as us. One day he had an accident and all the cans tipped out along the road. A woman passing by said, 'My poor man, have you had an accident?' He replied, 'No, Ma'am, just stocktaking.'

I had books and little treasures. I remember getting a handkerchief and I must have been very small because I was in a cot. It was a great big iron cot. And on it was pinned this little white handkerchief with a border of red roses and I thought it was the most beautiful thing I'd ever seen. A note said, 'To Ruby for being a good girl'. I couldn't even read but I remember somebody reading it to me. I was always being told I was naughty and it was one of the biggest surprises I ever got. It didn't say who it was from and I thought it was the fairies. Probably Auntie Bella bought it for me. Auntie Bella was very fond of me when I was a little girl.

One of my treasures was a miniature chest of drawers about six inches wide and eight inches high with long drawers and short drawers. All the front was different coloured little strips of wood. Uncle Peter Cameron bought it for me when I was about ten and I did treasure it. There were books my father gave me, one with a white kid cover and a blue kid band right down the back. I valued that a lot. We always had books, a lot of books. Mother was a great reader.

But they were stolen, with the brass candle sticks and the vases and the little chest of drawers. My mother left them all in two big boxes at my grandparents' house at Strahan when she moved round to Trowutta and someone came and knocked the end out of the house and took them. One of those boxes had come from Ireland with the Porteuses.

Mother had a beautiful vegetable garden. She was a good gardener. She had to be. There were some pockets of very good soil above the ironstone, among the clay and button grass. She used to do it all

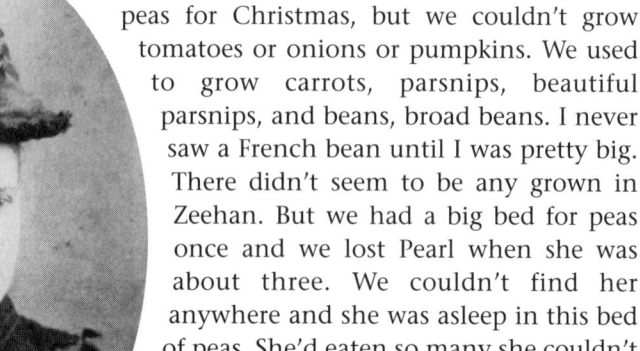

herself. You'd always have new potatoes and peas for Christmas, but we couldn't grow tomatoes or onions or pumpkins. We used to grow carrots, parsnips, beautiful parsnips, and beans, broad beans. I never saw a French bean until I was pretty big. There didn't seem to be any grown in Zeehan. But we had a big bed for peas once and we lost Pearl when she was about three. We couldn't find her anywhere and she was asleep in this bed of peas. She'd eaten so many she couldn't eat any more.

Cabbages grew beautifully. Huge they were! You never saw such cabbages! We always had big fields of them. The big white cabbage, that was named London Market, and in the wintertime we grew green curly Savoy. They were lovely. Lettuce and radishes too, and turnips. She used to grow the little white stone turnips and there was another one called Orange Jelly. It was just like that, only brown.

Ruby's mother, Emily Sophia Porteus

She had a lot of black currant bushes. They were beautiful black currants, bigger than peas. And a lot of gooseberry bushes. She always made gooseberry jam and black currant jam. We never grew strawberries. We put them in but you'd only get an odd one. We never had raspberries either, although other people did.

Mother used to buy potatoes by the bag at the auction market on a Saturday morning, where there were rabbits and bags of swedes and potatoes. She used to try to get a bag of swedes and a bag of potatoes, and that would do us quite a long time. She'd get them sent out with a carrier. We were at least three miles out. Now the road's straight, it doesn't seem so far in a car. I suppose when you are small and your legs are not very big it seems a lot longer.

Syl was very interested in the flower garden. She always kept it very nice. She had all the old-fashioned flowers, primroses and spring violets, mignonette, wallflowers. The wallflowers would be there for years. Foxgloves and lupins, Mother used to grow beautiful blue lupins. Poppies, but not a lot of annuals. Gladdies, they were left in the ground all the time. They were mostly red. And little golden lilies. 'Edith's curse' we called them. I think they were alstroemeria. We had roses, just the sort everyone had then, nothing like the roses now. The

Childhood home

big cabbage rose and white moss roses. There were two big poplars at the front gate. They were very tall and used to sucker. They were there as long as I can remember.

You don't realise at the time, but when I look back I realise we had a wonderful mother. She was almost more like one of the girls than she was a mother. Although we had to obey her. She got a stern voice on and that was it. 'Blow it' was swearing, but we were allowed to say 'Bother'.

She could sing and play, she was very well educated. She went to school in Dublin until she was seventeen and she learned French and painting as well as music. In Dublin she lived with this Auntie Maggie who was very gay and understanding. She was given everything in the world and Mother was very happy with her. She was the oldest and she was her father's favourite. Grandfather never

Ruby's father, Charles Alfred Pacey

denied her. He just worshipped her and she did him. When he was dying, he said, 'Emily, you've done everything for me all my life'. And she said, 'Yes, Father, and you've done everything for me and meant everything to me'. Grandma Porteus was all right, but Grandfather was easier to live with.

Emily came straight from school in Dublin out here to join her father. And after she left Ireland she never had any young life at all. She wasn't any age when she had four children. It was a tragedy really. She got married to Charles Pacey. He was the oldest of seventeen. But he was young and he'd never had any opportunities. I never knew much about his family. Really, none of them had much of a chance. Mother used to write to his mother, but he never wrote home. He always left it to Mother to do.

Chapter 3

Work and play

*"If we had a skipping rope we thought we were made ...
and if we had a ball that was something!"*

Ruby

When we came home from school we used to have to go and get wood. Once I saw my father come home and he went out into the bush. It was a long way out and he chopped a tree down, and cut it all up into wood. So we had this great big pile of wood, about ten or twelve ton in the yard, and each piece was five foot long. Mother had to cut it in half and split it, but it was wood and it was all there.

When it was getting down I said to Mother, 'I think we ought to go to the bush and get some wood, because this is nearly done'. But she said, 'You won't go to the bush while there's one stick of that wood there'.

She thought that it was a hardship for us to have to go and get two or three loads every night to carry on. But we loved the bush. There'd be waratah and beautiful pink laurel and about Christmastime the hills would be red with those bells, blandfordia.

Sometimes men would be cutting wood and chop all the limbs off a tree and leave them, so we'd cut them up and bring them home. We'd have an axe when we were big enough, but Mother often used to come of a Saturday with us and she'd find limbs amongst the trees. In the forest there was a big patch of manuka we called it, but it's also called paperbark. That was very good wood. In the summertime we used to get it if it had been washed down the river in the winter. We used to get another kind of manuka too, called teatree. That had a lot of oil in it and used to throw sparks when you put it on the fire. But it would burn no matter how wet it was. You could chop it out of the river and it would burn.

You'd see an odd snake by the river. We were a bit wary of snakes. If Mother was handy we'd sing out to her and she'd try to kill it. When we got a bit bigger we'd kill them ourselves. They weren't very big, not like those we got later at Trowutta.

We had about fourteen hives of bees. Mother used to take the honey and sell it, and make honey mead. Father used to make the bee boxes for us, with pointed roofs like little houses. We'd get the grocer to save us what we called salmon boxes – beautiful pine boxes that tinned salmon came in. My Grandfather Porteus used to make the frames for us. There were ten or twelve in each box. When you took out the frame sometimes they'd be joined together and that was a bad thing, because we had to cut the seal on them. Very choice parts we'd cut out and sell for honey in the comb.

Later on they had extractors, but Mother used to pound it all up. She used to buy a big chaff bag specially each year to strain it through and she'd always wash this bag and have it clean to put the honey in. And she'd mash it all up small. She had a big tub. She used to tie the bag of honey in the comb to a step of a ladder over this tub, and she would lean it up against the mantelpiece. It had to be a bit warm, but not hot, and she'd leave it for about a week to drain. And we'd keep scooping it out and selling it.

At the same time Mother had to use the fireplace for cooking, but you couldn't have a very big fire. When it was all drained out she'd wash all the wax, and the water from the washing made the honey mead. She put yeast into it. You could get drunk on it.

She'd boil the wax down in water in a kerosene tin and lift it off the top like you would fat off stock. You'd scrape all the bottom of it and might have to melt it down a couple of times to get it nice. Then she'd sell the wax. Beeswax and turpentine made the polish for the floor. It was shiny, but it was very hard work putting it on the boards or lino. By Jove it took some rubbing up.

Coming up to spring and summer we had to watch the bees. It was one child's job to watch them all day long and when they'd swarm we had a couple of old tin trays and dishes we used to bang with pieces of wood. Anything that made a noise 'd bring them down. Mother would come running out and follow the swarm across the button grass plain with a bucket of water.

If they were a bit difficult Mother would sprinkle water on them. In rain they'd make for the first bush. If she didn't get them then, she'd cover them with an old sheet until night and then she'd get a box ready. She used to wash the box out with honey and water to make it smell of honey and have it ready for a swarm. She'd put the frames in and then you'd just shake them down out of the bush.

Sometimes if the bees were difficult, Mother would put the box up over them, prop it up somehow. She had a thing she called a 'smoker' and when she was gathering a swarm, you'd puff it and that would sent them up into the box. This saved shaking them down, because you lose a lot that way. They get squashed.

All those years Mother worked with the bees she never came to any harm. Very seldom she got stung. There was just the blue bag and a bit of ammonia if you did get stung. When a bee stings you it leaves the sting in. If you pull it out, you squeeze the poison in. You try and straighten it out and it will come out naturally.

We had four cows – Betty, Nimble, Ratty, Poley and later on, Tulley. Ratty was always cranky. That's why Syl called her that. Nimble's milk always had a queer taste. I could never understand – she was always in good condition, yet she always had this same taste. They weren't any special breed. They were just cows on four legs. We didn't tether them, we just used to let them roam on the big grass along the road. We'd know which direction they went, we'd turn them in different directions. Sometimes my younger brother Bob used to have to get them in. We left them in a shed overnight and always fed them.

We put a big tin of water on the fireplace and when that was boiling we used to get what we called oil cake. It was made from the outside of coconut and it was in a hard cake. We'd soak it in the boiling water. Us kids often used to sneak a bit and it'd taste quite like coconut. Mother used to buy chaff and bran and she'd pour this boiling stuff over it. It used to be in a great big tub and you'd stir it all up with an old broomstick. Then she'd feed the cows. That's what they'd get, a big box every night. That and the grass they'd pick up and there were lots of things in the bush they could eat.

Mother milked them and made her own butter as well as selling the milk. She kept the cream cold in a cast iron bucket lined with enamel. It was the sort of bucket used by miners when they were tributing, that is working on contract with a mine. She made the butter with a ladle.

But it wasn't all work and no play for the children. In the yard there was a big clear patch where they'd taken the topsoil off, which would be about eighteen inches deep, and all the button grass, and left a big white patch of gravel, with a ledge around it and button grass tussocks as big and round as a chair. That was our shop.

We'd crumble up the black soil and that we sold as tea. And we'd get the big white stones, they were bread. The smaller stones were birds' eggs and chook eggs, different sizes of stones for different sorts of eggs. For ginger we'd get a big lump of yellow clay and scrape it all down with a knife, and the butter was big square pieces of clay. Our scales we made when Mother opened a new tin of kerosene. After she'd used the kerosene, she'd take the lid off it and make a handle, a little sort of loop in the middle. We used to turn the four corners in and we'd hold it by this loop and this was our scales, with a stone for a weight.

We used to get wax matches in little round tin boxes and then in little round cardboard boxes. We'd save the tops and bottoms and that was our money. Sometimes, if we didn't have them, we'd cut rounds out of paper. Quite a lot of people used to come over, fascinated with our shops. We used to pull the button grass off the roots and cut the stalks a couple of inches long and tie them in bundles and sell them for 'bread and butter'. And we used to eat them. They had to be very tender. Sometimes you could eat about three inches off the bottom. They were very nice. If they got old, they were tough. That would be our afternoon tea. Sometimes we'd have visitors. We would visit each other and be Mr and Mrs.

We used to play marbles and rounders and hopscotch. And if we had a skipping rope we thought we were made! If we could, we'd buy a sixpenny clothes line. If we didn't have a rope we'd tie some reeds together and they would last about three skips. If we had a ball it was just something! And we'd look after it too. A ball was the most treasured thing. They were just grey rubber. There were painted balls, but a grey ball was very strong and if you looked after it it would last you a long time.

If it was a wet day when we were little girls, they used to buy us a box of beads. It was as big as a matchbox, perhaps a bit bigger, and it had one big bead and lots of little ones in it. We'd make a couple of necklaces and rings and bangles. We'd thread them on cotton and they'd gradually break and we would pick them up but we wouldn't get them all. Some would roll away until they were all gone. They were a penny a box and we'd treasure them. There weren't children's necklaces much.

At Christmas we used to get a shilling doll. Sometimes they were stuffed with straw, sometimes with sawdust. Their legs would come off

Work and play

and you'd have to put them back on. They'd be worn out before next Christmas because we never had more than one doll between us. I wanted a doll when I was thirteen and Mother wouldn't buy it for me.

I remember one Christmas we were very poor. I don't know what my father was doing at that time. Perhaps he didn't have the money to send home. We got sixpence each. That was all the money they could scrape up. And Auntie Minnie gave us threepence. We girls bought a little doll each. We were such happy kids really.

button grass

There was four girls and two boys in our family and as we grew up there was a family of boys with one sister down the road from us. When the older ones got to be teenagers they got very friendly with us. We had a nice little sandy patch in front of our place. All around was tussocks and button grass. They made nice little seats if you opened them out, where we'd sit, and they'd be quite good for a long time.

These boys made what they called torches. They used to go to the slaughterhouse and get the discarded pieces of fat when they killed the bulls. They'd render them down. Then they used to wind a big piece of canvas round as big as a cup with three or four inches of canvas above the fat and then light them. They'd have two of these. The older boys used to play the accordion and they'd sit round on the button grass tussocks and sing. They had just started to work, and they used to bring fruit and lollies, and they'd sit around in front of these torches and sing. It was all right when Mother was home, because it was right in front of the window, and she'd come over and every now and again she'd join in.

Mother liked to supervise us always and she never liked this to go on when she wasn't home.

We used to play 'kick the tin'. You'd draw a base and you'd put an old tin in it. One would go 'he' and all the others would go and hide. He'd kick the tin as far away as he could and when he got it back to base sometimes he might have to count to twenty to give us all time to hide.

There was plenty of scrub and places to hide, but I suppose Mother thought it wasn't very proper for young girls to be hiding away with these boys. Whatever age they were, they were still boys! And Phyl and Syl were growing up. But when Mother went away we'd do it behind her back. She went to visit a neighbour one night, and there was too much laughter so she thought there was too much going on and she came back at a great rate! The boys all ran away as fast as they could go, but they came back again. They'd always come back again. They were a very nice family. But of course they were young men, and girls weren't allowed. It just wasn't done.

I got into trouble once. I did get into trouble! All because of hiding in a tree. When they cut down trees they put a 'shoe' in – a plank – and they climb up the tree on it and cut the tree off halfway up, leaving a very high stump, cut front and back. This tree in our yard had been felled and had split. I climbed up this stump to hide, and lo and behold, I only just got there when this Jack Brown came up. 'Would you keep quiet', he said and he was holding my head down. And the others were looking, they were looking everywhere. Mother must've come out and I was missing with Jack Brown!

I wasn't very old and we were right beside them really, in this stump. After a while, somebody heard me giggle. And my word! Mother went for me when they'd all gone. I got a terrible lecture, a real dressing down. And it wasn't my fault, because I went up there first!

Mother was a great reader and she used to read to the older children every night. *Mrs Wiggs of the Cabbage Patch*, *The Three Musketeers*, *For the Term of His Natural Life*, and we had all the Steele Rudd books. But I can beat any of them in real life! Books by Thomas Spencer and Bridget McSweeney too. When I was quite small she'd read a book. Then she'd say, 'Time for bed, you little ones. I'm not going to read any more'. And she'd put the book away until we went to bed.

But I loved all these books and I'd hear her reading another chapter and sometimes I'd sneak out of bed. There was a little passage between the living room and the bedroom with a little step. And I'd sneak out and sit on this step, and scuttle back to bed later. And sometimes she'd think she could go on the next night and we wouldn't know. But I'd always know. Small as I was, I'd know she'd missed something.

I used to tell my cousin Myrtle everything and I'd try to tell her about these books. I remember Mother reading once in *Robbery Under Arms* that they were coming along the track with a big mob. It was about cattle rustling. And I said to Myrtle, 'What's a mob?' I couldn't ask Mother because she would know then I'd been sitting on the step. The whole family was fond of reading and would read in bed by candlelight.

The paper, *The Zeehan and Dundas Herald*, used to be spread out in the windows of the newsagent and Myrtle and I used to go and read it there. There was one page of cablegrams, the overseas news, and we

Work and play

The Zeehan & Dundas Herald.

VOL. XIX.—NO. 107.   ZEEHAN, MONDAY, FEBRUARY 17, 1908.   PRICE: ONE PENNY.

used to read all that through the window. There was great rivalry between that and the Queenstown paper, *The Mount Lyell Standard*. They used to have a stock exchange in Queenstown on the street. And there were all the weekly papers. *The Weekly Courier* was printed in Launceston. But there was *The Australasian, The Leader*, and *The Bulletin*. They were really famous papers. I remember my father coming home once and he took us to a play. It was written up in the paper, '12 November, a night that all Zeehan will remember'.

I can only remember going to about two circuses and they were beautiful. The costumes were marvellous. Gerald's Circus was very famous. They used to pitch near the school – there was a big paddock near our school. And we used to go out at dinnertime and see the horses. They'd be practising. They'd always have a parade right up the street in full regalia to impress the people. Beautiful horses with bells, and their manes and their tails plaited up. This great big arena, it was really beautiful. It was covered with sawdust and the horses would dance to the music and these ladies would hop on and off, catch one and then jump off somewhere else. They were dressed so beautifully with things that sparkled all over them.

One night we had visitors. Phyl was engaged to Tom Hancock and he and his parents were spending the evening. The toilet was a couple of hundred yards away down the yard, so we had a chamber in the bedroom. Pearlie was a bit frightened – she wasn't very big – so she brought the po out on to the step in the light. And here were all these visitors dressed up, and the oldest sister already out at work with big ideas, and the young man courting!

Mother would sing of a night, nursing the youngest. She loved the old Irish songs, *Killarney, I'll take you home, Kathleen*, and *The Mountains of Mourne*. Sad songs too like *My Grandfather's Clock*. Sometimes she'd put on an old hat and sing comic songs, music hall songs. She used to play for square dances too, and the Irish jig, and polkas and mazurkas and quadrilles.

I remember when the Boer War started. We were on the coach going to Gormanston. I was inside the coach with Mother. It had two seats and they were as hard as anything, a sort of leather stuffed with horsehair. There was one across the front and one down each side, and then there'd be a couple of men on the box with the driver. We pulled up in Queenstown and Father got down off the front of the box when the coach stopped and he went back to Mother and he said, 'The Boer War has started'.

And I can remember when the Boer War ended and the men came home. The only one I can remember coming back to Zeehan was our schoolmaster's son, he must have been in the Light Horse. And we all met him at the station. He came on the train and they built a platform and we were to sing *God Save the King*. It was the King then. And nobody would sing, nobody would start. And the policeman standing there was that wild with these kids. He told us to go home.

I remember this soldier riding up the street in his hat and he looked over at his old home and he had to ride straight past. They had great big 'WELCOME HOME' banners that reached right across the street, and they gave him a great welcome. There were celebrations everywhere.

Everybody was having bonfires and we had one at our place. We carried all the brush and stuff from the bush and piled it up and there were crackers going off. The Brown boys came along and they brought most of the lollies we had. I was terrified of the crackers. Charlie, he must have been fourteen, was saying, 'Just hold this little tiny penny one. Look, I'll show you, it won't hurt'. And he'd hold it in his hand and it went off. He'd do everything.

I remember all the news coming through about the war, Mother reading it out of the paper, but I couldn't understand much. A little girl was born and they called her Pretoria. I remember the relief of Mafeking. And I can remember them singing *The Baby's Name Was*

Gaiety Theatre, Zeehan

Work and play

Kitchener. There were a lot of patriotic songs then – *The British Grenadiers, God Bless the Prince of Wales* and *Sons of the Sea*.

After we got our own money we'd go to the Gaiety Theatre. That's where we learnt skating. Skates then weren't like the skates today. You'd tie your skates and you used to screw them onto your shoes, a screw one on each side of your heel. Charl always had terrible smelly feet. He used to wash them and powder them before he'd go skating and we'd say, 'Look out, he's going to change his boots!'

There was the Academy of Music in the Gaiety Theatre and we had beautiful music. There was a German professor, Herr Hann, who used to play the piano, and an Austrian professor, Herr Mercer, he used to play the violin. He had the look of an old-time musician, his skin was very white and he was just different. He used to come out to our place and he used to teach Charlie the violin.

Sunday night there was nearly always what they called the Sacred Concert after church, with the best singers. The money probably went to the upkeep of the hall. And they had charity concerts – if anybody was burnt out, or somebody became a widow. We had a beautiful brass band too and a rotunda in the middle of the street on the hill. They used to play there. Mr Caddy was the bandmaster. Odd concerts we'd get to, if we were lucky, but not very often. Then there was the Corrick family – mother and father and Edie, Elsie and Ruby. Ruby Corrick had beautiful fair hair and she used to play a solid silver cornet.

When Dame Nellie Melba came to Zeehan, the first train after the railway from Mount Lyell was completed brought the miners through for the concert – down to Strahan and then up to Zeehan. Then it took them back and they had to go straight to work. In Zeehan there was a tram that ran right down the main street to the station. It was like a little engine. I wasn't very old when that stopped. That was for people. There were other trams that used to bring the ore out from the different mines.

I went to stay for about six months twice with mother's sister, Auntie Bella, at Gormanston, out of Queenstown. Father had his camp at North Lyell across the valley and worked in the mines there. Mother's brother Charl was a fitter and turner. He kept the works in order. Anything that broke down, he mended. He had an engine driver's certificate too, but I don't think he ever made much use of it. Auntie Bella's husband, Uncle Peter Cameron, was an engine driver at The Blow and leader of the Gormanston silver band. All the mining towns had bands. Miners in the early days were a wonderful lot of people.

The Queenstown hills were black with fumes from the smelters. Everything was black. The only patch of green was the sanitary dump way down near the King River. Kiddies used to take a few grains of wheat to school to grow in saucers – to learn how things grow. Gardens were impossible.

You could taste sulphur in the air and in the water. The sulphur was about eighteen inches deep. It was so thick that on a bad day clothes went the colour of a manila envelope. People wouldn't hang washing out on a bad day. People had china door knobs – sometimes brown, sometimes white with a flower – because metal ones crumbled in the fumes. Roofs were tarred twice a year and even then they would crumble. I got up on the ladder with Uncle Peter on the roof with a bucket of tar and a round brush on a long handle. And got a big blob of tar on my favourite dress! Painted roofs stood out like a sore thumb.

There used to be terrible wind storms. You couldn't open the front door for a whole week. The wind was a raging gale. A coach blew off the road over the hill from Queenstown once when Auntie Bella and cousin Jimmy were in it. And you've never felt anything so hot as the sun on the rocks. A terrible lot of people got burnt out. The sun would set the sulphur in the button grass alight and the peat under the button grass would burn eighteen inches deep. People would go into the mine tunnels if they could, to escape. One woman with a young baby went silly, and was silly ever after, poor thing.

It was very gay in Gormanston. They did everything there. We used to play nap nearly every night. You haven't lived until you've played nap. We played for pennies and ha'pennies. We used to have such fun and laughs. When I can't laugh I think I'll die. We always had supper and never went home before midnight.

I remember going to a circus in Queenstown. The same circus went to Strahan and my sister Phyllis had Pearl and Bob down there. Pearl was about four. They took her to the circus and when the elephant came in she said, 'There's a big pig with two tails'.

Everyone learnt music. There was skating to music. Someone played the piano. It was threepence for the afternoon and sixpence in the evening. Pearl was very good at skating. She had long legs and people used to say, 'Look out, here comes the ostrich!' They had to call her something because they gave everybody a nickname.

There was an Indian woman they used to call Old Mary. She was a hawker. She wasn't bad looking, she was dark, you know. She used to walk all over Queenstown and Gormanston. She used to carry this pack on her back done up in a big thing like a sheet. Her hands were twisted where she used to hang onto it on her shoulder. She'd open it out on the floor, and she'd have all these things to sell – buttons and combs and hankies and trinkets.

Work and play

There were four hotels in Gormanston then – two Ryans, Dennis Finnegan's, and Nicholls' Federal opposite the Post Office. If you went to the Rechabite social, you'd have to sign the pledge. Houses usually had two rooms and a skillion, and if they had a verandah they were flash.

Girls in Gormanston would earn two and sixpence a week dressmaking, or working in a shop. They married young and no married women worked. I left school when I was thirteen and went out to work looking after women having babies. The midwife would come twice a day for the first couple of days to fix up the mother and bath the baby, and the girl would mind the other children, make the meals, wash the linen and the nappies and everything. I was a real good washer and I always kept the laundry floor clean. You'd get eight shillings a week, perhaps six, or sometimes even ten if you were very well paid. I did that for a couple of years.

Descendants of William and Eliza Porteus.
The Pacey family. Emily Sophia with her adult children. L–R: Emily (Phyllis), Sylvia, Pearl, Ruby. Front: Robert (Bob), Emily Sophia, Charles (Charl), about 1940

Chapter 4

The Porteus family

"There's never a day goes by but that I learn something new."

Ruby's mother's parents, William and Eliza Porteus, were a very important part of her childhood. After coming out to Tasmania from Ireland in the 1880s, they moved from Hobart to Strahan on the West Coast to be nearer to their married daughters, Ruby's mother, Emily Sophia, and Minnie at Zeehan. Ruby soaked up the stories of life in Ireland, told in their warm Irish brogue, and loved to recount anecdotes about them all her life.

Ruby

Grandfather and Grandmother Porteus lived up on a high hill at Strahan, and Grandfather had a whalebone on each gatepost marking the entrance to the fern log path to the house. They split the big man fern logs in half and made a path of them right from the gate. They had an arch with white roses halfway up and further up again they had what they used to call 'the picket'. It was a pit in a half circle and the house was on one side. On summer evenings they'd sit out there. From there you could look out over the ocean and see the lighthouse, and we used to watch that for hours. I remember these big green and red lights coming on and going off all night long. It was a lovely place.

arum lilies

There were big clumps of arum lilies and Grandfather had a couple of boronia bushes. Some of the kids that used to come up from Strahan used to pick his boronias, so he enclosed them in a wire netting cage, because he liked the scent of them in the garden.

He'd work away in his garden, and when he'd see you coming he'd drop his tools and stand up and he'd wave to you, saying, 'Welcome, Ruby! Welcome, Pearl!' *Purrl* he always said it. Pearl was his favourite. He loved Pearl because she lived with them a good bit when they were at Strahan. He often called us 'Daughty'. That was a pet name. And when we went to bed he'd say, 'Quit the laughing and quench the candle'.

Pearl learnt to make a sponge cake when she was about eight or nine. Grandma Porteus taught her and she was allowed five eggs. We thought this was terribly extravagant. Pearl used to whip up this cake and what a mess she made!

William Lee and Elizabeth Porteus, parents of Emily Sophia, grandparents of Ruby, Golden Wedding portrait 22 March 1916

Gran Porteus made soda bread too, great big loaves of it. It was beautiful. It was a bit yellow, she used to put a fair bit of soda in it. They were lovely, especially when they were still hot, with butter. They were more cakey than scones. She made them with the buttermilk and soda and cream of tartar. She just rolled them in a ball and then patted them a bit. They weren't cooked in a tin, they were just cooked on the shelf.

Grandfather used to tell us stories and they believed them. They said that all over Ireland there were little folk. But they were frightened to go near the forts on the hillsides or the tunnels, for fear of disturbing them. They were too superstitious. Grandma said, 'When I was little everywhere there was a fort, from one hill to another was connected. I've seen fairies, but they're not there now'.

They had some sayings. 'Ta polla richa' Granny would say if she was talking and didn't want somebody to hear. It didn't matter if it was children or adults. That's what it sounded like. Like we'd say 'little pigs have big ears'.

Grandma Porteus brought out her goosedown quilts from Ireland. Yes, and I've still got a mattress ticking they'd spun themselves. Linen it was. Perhaps they even grew the flax. It was as thick as a board and as cold as ice and it wore into little pinholes. It was a bed tick filled with down. And when it got older we had to fill it up with kapok. Grandma Porteus used to talk about how from the age of twelve the girls used to save the down to make the quilts for their dowry. They'd pluck the goose's breast and then they'd let it go.

A goose feather bed was lovely to sink into. You'd shake it up and it'd be that high. Of course it's half kapok now. Once I nearly lost it. There was going to be a strike at Rosebery and there were a couple of agitators there. The women were going to tar and feather them and they wanted my tick. Lucky I just happened to come home in time!

There was a patchwork quilt Grandma had made too, all beautiful colours, jewel colours. Bits of silk, red, a gorgeous red, and bits of velvet, rich blue. There was lots of velvet. Beautiful velvet. It had a feel all its own. Little bits and odd shapes of everything all featherstitched together, with a big velvet diamond in the centre. And she always knew what they'd been in before. In the end it was absolutely worn out and Pearl pulled it apart and gave the patches to my youngest daughter Lilian to play with. Lilian kept them in her little sewing box and called them 'My patches'.

And there was a woolwork picture of a parrot Grandma Porteus made when she was sixteen. They grew the wool and dyed it themselves. It's got the most gorgeous colours in it and it's never faded. Gran said, 'And I counted every thread'. In Ireland they used to spin and weave their own cloth and her mother used to keep these bolts of cloth and linen in big balsa chests. Granny used to play the Lady Bountiful and go down into the village and dispense them to the poor people. And her mother would go to get some cloth to make dresses and find that it was mostly all gone. Grandma used to make all the clothes for her sons by hand. She never thought of a machine. Will, her eldest son, had his first bought suit to come out from Ireland. He was seventeen or eighteen then.

Grandma's sister Maggie was very much the opposite to her. She was fond of life and she just loved a joke. William (Grandpa Porteus) had proposed to Eliza (Grandma) three times. But she wouldn't give him an answer. Maggie was very keen on Will and she said to her sister, 'If you don't marry William Porteus, I will'. So Eliza went and married him.

Grandpa and Maggie got down in the bog with sheets over them and were making noises like ghosts. They did this several times, night after night, and they had all the men at the hotel terrified of these ghosts down in the bog. So the men decided they'd have a hunt one night and things got pretty serious, so William and Maggie had to call it off. They were not game to do it again. I don't think it was ever found out who it was. But Granny would have been shocked. She was that type of person, so much the opposite.

Everybody was playing up in Ireland and Sinn Feiners were active. Granny was walking out one day and she saw two men running along the road, trying to hide behind the bushes. She came to a bridge and she was just going through the gate and she said, 'I didn't look at them. I just said, 'There's four soldiers, four or five soldiers, coming along on horses, if it means anything to you'. They just went down under the buttress of the bridge and the fellows rode on.

She didn't want to come to Australia. She said, 'I cried and I cried'. She used to cry, of course she did, because she didn't know anybody here and she was homesick. And she said, 'I ran out into the hedges'. And she gathered up pieces of fuchsia. And she said, 'I brought them with me and planted them'. I reckon there's still some growing out there at Strahan. And we had it at Trowutta. We had a lot of it there. It was growing all amongst the pine trees, it was everywhere there at Trowutta. At Strahan we kids used to get out and pop the buds.

fuchsia

Every night before she went to bed she used to like to go out and view the heavens. And she'd say, 'Listen, Ruby, you'll hear the grass grow. It goes click, click, click'. I said one night, 'Granny, I can hear the grass grow'. But whether it was the grass I heard or not, I don't know. She always said she could hear the grass grow. And she'd look all around the sky. She always looked around the sky, and she could see the pattern of an emu. I can see it now occasionally. It was just like a big darker patch. If it was very cloudy you wouldn't see it. You'd only see it on a clear night. And she'd say, 'It's going to be a fine day tomorrow'.

Grandma Porteus had a big heavy silver teapot she brought out with her too. It's made tons of pots of tea. It was about an inch taller than it is now. But someone sat it on the stove and the bottom melted out. I had another bottom put on it, but it didn't have the quality. She always had a big brass bowl with buttons and corks in it on the end of the mantelpiece. It had all sorts of buttons. There used to be such pretty buttons, and we used to love it. She'd give it to us to play with and we'd put them all out on the table.

She always read her Bible every night. She used to use a milk tin and polish it up and that's what she used to stand on her Bible as she'd be reading it. She'd have the Bible open and she'd always have a penny story book in it. She'd turn a page over and put the milk tin on it, but she always had the penny story in it. Grandpa loved any sentimental old story. 'Oh, man,' he'd say, 'begad and he was a bad fellow that'.

She was a wonderful old lady to us when we were in Zeehan and we were poor. She'd come up and rescue Father from his troubles. He hated the sight of her. But she always said she learnt something every day of her life. She said, 'There's never a day go by but that I learn something new'.

Once she was staying in Zeehan with her daughter Minnie, who was married to Joe Smith. Uncle Joe had these very valuable pigeons. Pigeon racing was very popular. They used to put the pigeons in a box and give them to the guard on the train and he'd let them go out at Renison Bell or Farrell's Siding or Tullah, and the pigeons would all fly home and get in their lofts. When they came home they would land on a little trapdoor into the loft. Their owners had to catch them and then they'd have runners to take the pigeons to a certain place in Zeehan to check them in.

Uncle Joe used to get that excited he'd be shaking, but Ted Sawley – Ted was a pretty good runner – he'd never let Joe go far. He'd take the bird next and do the longest run, and then somebody else would meet him. And whoever got to the checkpoint first, their bird won the race. It was very exciting really.

Anyway, Uncle Joe was on afternoon shift and Auntie Minnie was in bed sick and Granny Porteus was reading her Bible. She said she felt somebody watching her through the window and she felt all night there was an eye on her. So she said she took a candle and went outside and looked all round a couple of times because she felt there was those eyes watching her. She said she knew there was somebody there.

When Uncle Joe came home she told him and he went out to the pigeon loft and his bird was gone. They'd taken it to breed from.

Our Porteus ancestors had come from Scotland to Ireland originally. Auntie Mollie Jones, my mother's cousin, told us, 'That book *The Three Musketeers* is really based on fact. Those people really existed.' She said Porthos was killed and she said one escaped and he fled to Ireland and he took the name Porteus. And she said that's where they originated. My eldest daughter Madge said, 'That's a lot of rot'. I don't know how true it is. I suppose they were scoundrels and some got into the church. Mr Dowling, the Church of England minister at Strahan, said they were a lot of scoundrels and so were his people, but they weren't such big scoundrels as the Porteuses.

A lot were Archdeacons in the Church of England and Grandfather was supposed to be a parson, but he wouldn't. He was a tenant farmer at Lisdrumgran in County Leitrim. But the land was poor and the landlords kept raising the rents. He came out to Australia on the *Lusitania* and arrived in Tasmania on the *Ringarooma* in 1882. Grandma stayed at home with her parents in Ireland, with the children. They owned a house and property called Bellevue at Carrick on Shannon. The children used to make ropes of hay and swing out over the river.

Grandpa was working in the brick trade in Hobart, for a man named Waller. My mother, she was their oldest child, came out on the *Iberia* and arrived in Hobart in 1885. She met my father, Charles Pacey, and they married the next year. She was nineteen. Her brother Will arrived in 1886. Grandma came out in 1889 with John and Minnie, but left the two youngest, Bob and Bella with her parents, to finish their education. It was nearly ten years before they got here – Bob in 1898, and Bella in 1899 when she was nineteen.

Grandpa Porteus started up this farm at Strahan, but the bush was so thick you couldn't get your hand between the trees. They had a milk run in Strahan. Everything used to come from Hobart on the steamer to Strahan in the early days. My mother's brothers, Uncle Will and Uncle Jack, had packhorses and they used to take goods up to Queenstown for the shops. And they used to meet the cattle which came into Strahan on the train by the Emu Bay Railway from Burnie on the north coast. They'd drive the cattle up the corduroy track to Queenstown. It took two days to walk them up, riding a horse, sleeping overnight on the button grass plains.

Uncle Jack was ninety when he told the story of the beach whisky to the paper, but we all knew it of course, even though we kids weren't supposed to. I heard it from my cousin Myrtle. She was staying at Strahan with our grandparents and she'd always listen in to what the older people were talking about. You'd see her putting her hands behind her ears and listening, and she knew everything, she just knew everything. They'd been to Strahan and she whispered to me – we were just being put to bed – 'Don't go to sleep,' she said, 'I've got something to tell you'.

There were so many of us. There were three at the head of the bed and two at the foot. We got in together of course, which we always did, and she told me the story of how it happened.

There was a wreck. The *Kawatiri* was wrecked and a terrible lot were drowned. The lighthouse keeper out at Hell's Gates, he'd only just been sent there. And his wife and child were on this ship. He could hear her calling out to save her, but he couldn't leave his post. And she was drowned, her and the baby. They saved a good many but there were two babies drowned. They got the body of one baby and both lots of parents wanted to claim it and bury it.

It was about a week afterwards when Uncle Jack and Bob Ward were going out to the hut on their cattle run. And they saw this cask of whisky on the beach. So between them they rolled it over to a sandbank and tipped all the sand down over it. They went home, got a horse and cart and a few slabs of timber ... and I'll tell you what villains they were.

They went and got the whisky, brought it home and thought nobody knew anything about it. And then they got the whisky up to the farm about two miles up the Lyell road. Bob Ward went to have a drink at the pub and they were all talking about this cask of whisky that was floating out on the ocean. It'd been seen and someone had reported it to the police. They went out in a boat and couldn't find it.

So Bob came rushing back and he and Uncle Jack went and dug a hole in a paddock, buried the whisky and threw ferns over it.

The police went down the beach and saw the tracks. Uncle Jack had protectors all over his boots and they could see the marks in the sand. So up came Sergeant Lonergan and the two policemen they'd got from Zeehan to search for it. They hated this sergeant. He was their superior. He was a great big man and he used to walk with his hands behind his back. He walked along and they walked behind him, and the two policemen walked right over it and never squeaked a word. They never let on, but Uncle Jack swears they knew. They never ever told him they did, but they got a fair share of the whisky.

Well, Uncle Jack was cunning enough. He knew he had these boot protectors and he took them all out and rubbed mud in his boots. He took them out altogether – no use turning them the other way. There was toe plates and heel plates, and other little ones that used to go down. They were three-cornered and some were round. They were just all shapes for different parts of the sole.

Sergeant Lonergan met him down the street and said, 'Well, you've got that whisky, Johnny, you know very well you got the whisky'.

And Uncle Jack said, 'Did I? Well,' he said, 'you've got to prove it, haven't you? I've never seen any whisky'. It was overproof whisky. It had to be diluted. And it was a big cask. So it was very valuable.

'Well,' Sergeant Lonergan said, 'show me your boots'.

So Jack proudly pops up his boots. He was on a horse and he pops up his boots to show the sergeant.

There was a big piece in the paper then about the beach whisky and it ended up that Sergeant Lonergan thought he'd found a mare's nest. 'Not there, my child, not there ...' there was a poem in our books, you know, about a child asking her mother all these questions about heaven and every verse ended, 'Not there, my child, not there'.*

One day Grandfather was going round with the milk. There were a couple of fellows on the hotel verandah and they said to him, 'Now, what about a drop of the beach whisky?' And they thought they were going to get a bit. So Grandfather he got down off his horse and took the lid off the milk can and he said, 'Not there, my child, not there'.

They came up to search the farm, and the sergeant, he made Grandfather go with him. Grandfather had a few possum skins out of season drying on a board on top of the dairy. So he said, 'Well, I'll have to go back and get my coat'. When he went back, he beckoned Granny into the bedroom and said, 'Get rid of those possum skins while we're away'.

Sergeant Lonergan took Grandfather with him and they searched all the sheds and everywhere. Lonergan was sure he'd find the whisky. But by then the soil had settled. So they came back, Grandfather and Sergeant Lonergan, from searching everywhere, sheds and all the old trees and poking everything round about.

'Well,' the sergeant said, 'I saw a couple of possum skins. Where are they?' he said. 'I saw them up there.'

Grandfather said, 'Possum skins? Here? We wouldn't have any possum skins. No'.

And the sergeant couldn't find the possum skins because Granny had taken them. They had a pig sty in a hollow tree. It was a very high tree that had had about three shoes put in it, and over the top of it was a galvanised iron roof, just hammered all round down the tree. And Granny had got the skins and the clothes prop and she prodded those skins right up to the top of the hollow tree while Grandfather was gone. So of course they couldn't find the possum skins either. They'd left it a bit late.

---

* From the poem 'The Better Land' by Mrs Felicia Hemans.

The Porteus family

There was an old house about two miles further up the Lyell road and Uncle Jack and Bob Ward were sure a couple of detectives were there. They knew these fellows were watching them. So during a terrible storm they waited until the middle of the night and they dug up the whisky. Uncle Jack strapped the axe to his back. He said, 'They won't get it anyway. If they catch me, I'm going to put the axe into it'.

It was an awful night, hail, lightning and gales, and they took it way over between two hills. They'd prepared the place and they had to roll it nearly all the way. And that's where it stayed for six months before they did anything with it.

The hotel-keepers in Zeehan were after it, they all wanted some. They came down from Zeehan on the train. So Uncle Jack and Bob Ward sold it and got rid of a good lot of it and drank a lot of it. Even the hotel-keepers didn't like this old Sergeant Lonergan and they'd advertise 'Beach Whisky', you know. They'd put it up, 'Best Beach Whisky'.

I was frightened the next morning after I heard the story from Myrtle. I had to go to Sergeant Lonergan's with the milk. He'd never spoken to me in his life and that morning he said to me, 'What's your name?'

And I said, 'Ruby Pacey'.

And he said, 'Ah, and a great girl you are'. He was Irish, you see. 'And Johnny Porteus is your uncle, isn't he?'

I was frightened to tell Mother because I wasn't supposed to know anything about it. So I said, 'I don't want to go to Sergeant Lonergan's with the milk'.

'Oh,' she said, 'You just have to go'.

Anyway, he never said anything else to me at any other time, but that morning he did. You can imagine how frightened I was, because I would've been too frightened not to tell him.

After Sergeant Lonergan retired he went to Hobart to live, and his son had a shop near my Auntie Minnie's house. Her daughter was in the shop one day and she asked him, 'How's your father these days?'

'He's pretty good', he said.

And she said, 'Ask him, does he remember the beach whisky?'

So next time Auntie Minnie's daughter went in, he said, 'What in the name of God was the beach whisky? The old fellow nearly jumped up to the ceiling!'

I think he never got over it, that poor old Sergeant Lonergan.

Grandpa was very devout and when he was dying, he said the Father and the Son came and stood by his bed, one on each side, and he said, 'I'll never complain again'. And he never did. He had pleurisy and if they'd have drained the fluid off him I don't think he'd ever have died.

My family were very long livers. Grandfather was ninety when he died and Grandma was ninety-five. Auntie Minnie was eighty-three, Mother was eighty-four and Auntie Bella was eighty-five. Uncle Will died a week before his ninety-third birthday. Uncle Jack was ninety-four. Uncle Bob, he was the only one that died young. He was gored by a bull and he died early. He was only seventy-five.

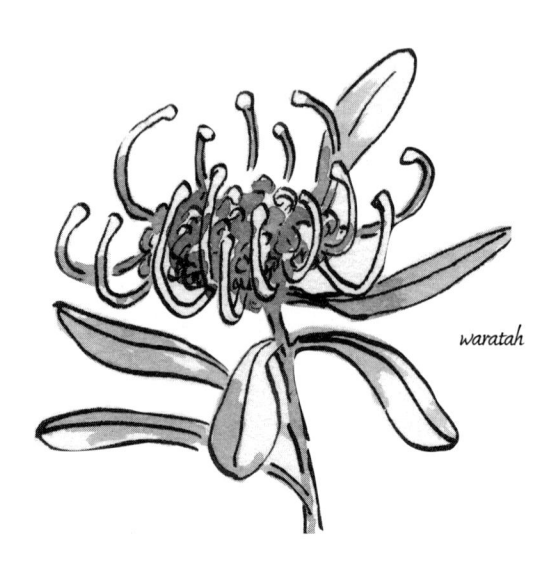

waratah

Chapter 5

A wedding to remember

"All done up like fried bread!"

Ruby was fifteen when she left Zeehan. Her sister Phyllis had married and moved to Moina, a small mining settlement in the North-West. She asked Ruby to stay. After her brother-in-law became ill, Ruby remained to help with the children.

Her father had been forced to leave mining after contracting the dreaded disease, phthisis. He bought a farm in Scotchtown where he was joined by Emily, whose parents then moved from Strahan to Trowutta to be close to their daughters. Ruby's father died in June 1915 and was buried in the Scotchtown cemetery.

Ruby was twenty-one when she became housekeeper at Kilranelagh, a Scotchtown property owned by the Greens, with a beautiful old house and garden. There she met her husband-to-be, Colin Paul, the farm overseer. Perhaps that is why Ruby always remembered Miss Green saying, 'Kissing a man without a moustache is like eating an egg without salt'. Ruby married Colin in 1916.

Ruby

I got married in a hurry! We had just got to Trowutta. I was going to be married on June 24th 1916. But my father had died. He left the West Coast and came to Scotchtown when his health was breaking down. He had miners' consumption from getting dust on the lungs. So we brought Grandmother and Grandfather Porteus round from Strahan to live with Mother.

I remember poor old Granny Porteus saying, 'That girl needs a tonic before she gets married'. So she got some Peruvian bark and port wine, and gave me a glass every night. Peruvian bark, if you've ever tasted it, well, it'll never make a drunkard of you. It's as bitter as gall. And port wine. I hate the smell of it, any alcoholic smell!

It was Grandma and Grandpa Porteous's Golden Wedding on 22nd March. So it was decided Col and I should be married when all the family gathered on that day, instead of 24th June. So we had to get married in a hurry! I didn't have any clothes or anything. I had my wedding dress and that was all. I didn't know whether I was married or not. The parson was the Reverend Middleton McDonald. He'd been in India for years so he'd never married a white couple and he was that excited he forgot things.

You didn't have big weddings. Ours was big enough for the house, because the house was only just finished. It was just four rooms and there was no verandah, no anything. We didn't have much furniture. I made a dresser out of a heap of palings and papered it with wallpaper. We had some furniture on the West Coast and we got that round afterwards. So that's what we had. There wasn't a bit of garden. We had sliprails for a gate and all this raw sort of clay where the house was just built.

My sister Pearlie was the bridesmaid. Uncle Will or Grandfather gave me away. Uncle Will and Uncle Bob, Grandfather's and Grandma's sons, were on a farm over at Mount Hicks. There was a big sale and they had to sell these cattle, and they wrote and said they couldn't come. So Granny Porteus sat down and she wrote to them. 'Well, for all your cattle sale,' she said, 'if we were dead, you'd come. And we don't want you when we're dead. We want you now'. So Uncle Will came and Uncle Bob stayed. Some of Colin's people came from Melbourne too. Colin Cattanach Paul was his name. Old Grandma Paul was related to Madam Melba, second or third cousin to the Mitchells.

We were to be married at half-past eight in the morning and we invited nearly everybody in Trowutta. We didn't have quite enough room to invite everybody. All these people milked their cows and they'd just had a cup of tea. The wedding breakfast was going to be their breakfast. We had a big kitchen and that was where the wedding breakfast was laid out.

I was all dressed up like fried bread and I had my wedding veil and my orange blossoms on. I didn't know how to put the veil on. I suppose we should have fixed it before, but we didn't have a dress rehearsal. My wedding dress was a silk striped voile, a fancy stripe

A wedding to remember

cream woollen voile, with a narrow little satin stripe. It had a basque hooked onto the back of my bodice. The basque hung down below the hipline and had this beautiful wide silk fringe. It was really beautiful, that fringe.

And I had a pair of white shoes that I'd borrowed. I'd never had a white shoe on me in my life before. They were Mrs Dave McDonald's. She was married to Col's cousin. They had a farm at Trowutta. She couldn't come to the wedding because she was going to have a baby. Mind you, that's how they were in those days. She was so excited over the wedding she lent me her white shoes. I can't remember whether I had white stockings. I suppose I did. I wouldn't have worn black stockings, would I? I suppose they were her stockings too.

Ruby Alice Pacey before her marriage

Then the bridegroom didn't turn up!

We waited and we waited, then everybody was hungry. So Mother had to give them half the wedding breakfast. Way out there we didn't have that much. You couldn't afford to feed ten or eleven people for breakfast and then have enough for the week. Anyway, she did the best she could. She kept giving them cups of tea.

They had me sitting in the bedroom, wouldn't let me come out. I suppose they thought it wasn't proper for the bride to be seen by all and sundry. So I put my head round the door and said, 'I'm hungry'. And Mother brought me a plateful of chicken. I wasn't worried. I did know Col would turn up.

He did, but not till a quarter to twelve!

I can see the old parson now coming in. He came out the night before and stayed with some friends, Mr Brydges, because the road wasn't too good. It was the parson that was getting in a fuss. He was getting flustered because the bridegroom hadn't arrived and there were no telephones, and if there was, Mrs Frost had the post office closed because she was at the wedding. It was my brother Bob's birthday, and we had my niece Minnie Sawley baptised too. And this old parson said he sent the story of that wedding to every paper in Australia and everywhere I went people knew about it. Everybody said, 'Oh, that's the wedding we read about'.

When Col eventually turned up, he'd had to push the car all the way up to Trowutta from Irishtown, about fifteen miles.

There were only three motors in Smithton – two big open motor buses and only one car, a T Ford. It was Show Day at Wynyard along the coast and these two buses had gone to the Show. And this poor old man, Joey Morton, he used to drive horses, and they left him to bring the car! And he couldn't get it to go. He had to bring Col out from Irishtown and he couldn't get it to go. And here was Col waiting and waiting and waiting, and the car didn't turn up.

So Col thought, 'Well, I'll ride out and get married'. So he got on his horse and about two miles along the road old Joey came along in the car.

So Col had to ride back and put his horse away.

Joey said, 'I've had terrible trouble to get it to go. But now I've got it going there's no stopping it'. They got to the first hill and the car stopped. It wouldn't go up the hill. It was a real steep hill, a mile long. There was an old fellow splitting sleepers on the side of the road. So Col got out and this fellow came along and every so often he'd drop a sleeper in to stop the car going back. And Col pushed it right up the hill. When they got to the top it went down all right and they got a little way. Joey got out 'to screw its tail' and Colin said, 'For goodness sake, don't stop it while it's going'.

Joey said, 'It won't stop now'. Anyway, he got out and it wouldn't go at all. Colin had to push it all along the flat road and all up the Trowutta Hill from Roger River. A lot of the road was not metalled. It was yellow clay and dirt.

So when Colin got to Trowutta he was filthy. He was in a sweat. And he'd had a nose bleed as well. His shirt and everything was dirty. He had a tucked shirt – everything he got was very good – five tucks each side, big tucks, with a starched front. He wore a pale grey lavender tie. He'd got a new suit to get married in and everything was dirty. He had to go and have a wash.

The old parson was that pleased to see him and said, 'We'll give the young man a few minutes to compose himself'. And he went where Col was having his wash and asked Col for the fee. He told these other parsons afterwards, 'He must have valued his bride a bit more than most people. He gave me a pound extra!'

Col had a good wash and then they found that the parson had forgotten his book and Grandfather had to find one. But we got married eventually. I think we did! We got married and ate what was left of the wedding breakfast. I remember there was some beautiful Jonathans. Colin was terrible fond of apples. He'd eat them like a cow chewing a swede. He wouldn't even leave the pips. So he took two of these apples in his pockets.

All I had to go away in was a black costume. Of course everybody thought that was all right because my father had died. But I didn't think it was much. My sister Phyl tried to make it a bit smart. She put a belt fastened at the back with a big fancy button and every time I sat down this button stuck into me. I had to cut it off before I got too far.

And I didn't have a coat at all. My grandmother lent me a coat for my honeymoon, so that's that. There was me in my grandmother's coat, a charcoal grey sort of gaberdine sewn up the front so you put it on over your head. Nothing took any getting into in those days. You just threw them on. You didn't stand preening. It was a bit long for me, but it was a very nice coat. But I will tell you what I did have in my trousseau. A beautiful pair of blue cashmere stockings, saxe blue. They came from Scotland and they were given to me.

We went out to get in the car. And it wouldn't go! And there we were getting pelted with rice through the torn side curtains. Anyway, a whole lot of men got hold of the car and pushed it up the top of Cameron's Hill and that's how we started. Once they got us to the top, the car never stopped again.

After we left they had the great shivoo. They christened the baby and had the party for my brother Bob's birthday. I suppose they scooped up the rice and made a few more scones. There would've been enough chicken. All sorts were killed for the wedding.

We came right into Smithton and as a great favour we had to pick up Hoppy Nichol. (Hoppy had a cork leg. He joined the Brethren and when they went to baptise him, they couldn't get him under the water.) Anyway, we had to go to the bank and we had to pick this man up. And then catch the boat from Stanley to Melbourne for our honeymoon.

We were to be married at half past eight – that's why it was early – to catch the *Marrawah*. It was to go out at eleven o'clock and it waited until nearly two for us. Then off it started for Melbourne.

When our car came round the hill to Stanley, the boat saw us and started to blow its horn and come back. It came right back to the wharf blowing its siren and everybody was shooting windows up and running out. They put the gangway down and I came running with a bandbox in one hand and I don't know what else, rushing to get on.

On the boat was a Mrs McLaughlin. Mr McLaughlin was a funny old fellow. He married a widow and they had 'your kids, my kids and our kids'. Anyway, this day she had only a baby with her and she was sick. I suppose she was going to have another baby and she was terrible sick. She was dropping the baby and I would catch it. Col went to find the stewardess and there was I left with this baby nearly all the way on my honeymoon night, holding this baby and the poor woman. They got her down into her bunk and left me with the baby! That's the dinkum truth. I was born to have things happen to me!

Ruby Pacey and Colin Paul, wedding portrait, 22 March 1916

Anyway we went to Victoria and met all Colin's people. And when we came home it was pouring with rain and terrible cold and we went to the Coffee Palace in Smithton for a meal. And the parson jumps up, 'Oh, here's the bride and bridegroom!' And everybody came running to see the bride and bridegroom and I was still in my old black. They all rushed round me and the old fellow said, 'You've got to sign your name again as Miss Pacey. We didn't do the papers right'.

So that's why I didn't think I was married! I reckon I lived in sin all that time!

Chapter 6

Scotchtown

"We had no roads."

Ruby

In the early days every district had a progress association. Very early, before Father died, before the big fires in 1914, Roger River and Trowutta folk wanted roads. The roads we had were very bad. Parts had never had anything done beyond patches. They'd pick a stretch thought to be worst in summer and put on a bit of gravel. But it would be hardly possible to get over the next hundred yards. And they wanted a railway. We wanted roads and a railway.

They'd written to Hobart asking the politicians to come and see the potential of the district, sawmills, blackwoods and the roads, and the prospects for opening up this country. Eventually the politicians decided to come. They had a four-in-hand to bring them out from Smithton.

There was a couple of reporters and six or eight politicians, all dressed up. Poor old Joey Morton, that couldn't drive the car when we were married, he was driving this four-in-hand, and they came to this awful big pool of mud and water and the horses wouldn't tackle it. So the men all had to get out. There were logs right up the side and they clambered along them for about a hundred yards.

Joey had to take his leggings and boots off and turn his jodhpurs up to lead the horses through. And when he got them in they were plunging everywhere. We had just come along on our horses. That's how I know so much about it. Well, by the time they got through they'd stirred it up and made it so much worse. But we got through all right because we could sidetrack a bit with our horses.

When they got to the bottom of Trowutta Hill it was just too bad to go up with a four-in-hand. So they met them with a bullock dray and took them up right to the far end of Trowutta, on to the little house that we bought later, where they had the meeting and a big banner up about the Trowutta road and railway. After they'd seen the roads it was as if they heard 'cries from the earth'. They made speeches and we had our photo taken. There was a photo of the boy too who walked the bullocks with the wagon up Trowutta Hill and he was mud from head to foot. Then they were feasted. Everybody cooked, but there wouldn't be any beer. Then they had to stay the night. And it was only a little house. I don't know how they fitted them in.

Next morning going down Spinks Hill, that was dreadful. One of the reporters was in a jinker and the going was so bad and the mud so stiff that it broke the tugs of the jinker and it tipped up backwards. This reporter, he was only a little man and he had a suit of browny Donegal tweed and a bowler hat, and all you could see was his legs sticking up in the mud!

Afterwards they did get a big grant on the roads and that was when they started to talk about the railway. At that time the railway came through a bit further than Boat Harbour, to Myalla. So then they brought it right through, first to Stanley and then out to Trowutta. It was a great boon. It did a lot for Circular Head. It opened up the country. It came from Burnie right through to Irishtown. There was a Y junction at Wiltshire Junction and the Trowutta train came straight out through Irishtown. It used to get in late at night. Smithton was a branch line. It ran every day. At one time it was the only paying line in Tasmania. It used to take all the produce – there was a lot of potatoes and swedes grown, and a terrible lot of sawmills. That's when they sent a lot of timber to Melbourne from Stanley. The train went straight from Trowutta to Stanley. Before we were married we went to some big do, the turning of the sod, when they laid the foundation stone. It wasn't finished until years after, till about 1921.

When the First World War started the Army took men aged up to forty-five. Will Porteus, Harry and Burley Butler, Harold and Norman Sawley, Arthur Crole and his father went from the district. Mr Crole had a big family and he was very loyal. They had a hard struggle on the farm. First of all the son Arthur put his age up and went to the war. Then the father went. He was looking forward to being a soldier and they made him a lieutenant. He was leading his men and just as they were going into battle his head was shot off.

Arthur had been gassed and he was in England and they let him come home to his mother because she was widowed and had this big family and a farm. She got a pension for losing her husband, but Arthur had to forego all his rights as a soldier and he never got anything. In the Second World War he got a commission training soldiers, but he never got anything for the First. We had a patriotic fund and we did a lot of things to raise money during the war. After the Second World War they had a big do in the district and they bought every man a watch.

Ted Sawley had two brothers killed in the First World War – Harold and Norman. It broke their father's heart. He used to sing out at night that Norman wasn't buried. Harold went away with the first attendance. The ship they were on had a submarine after it as they approached the Bay of Biscay and they were zig-zagging all the way. They didn't think they'd ever get in.

When we left the old house in Zeehan we had a tenant for a little while. Then Mother arranged for Myrtle's husband Harold, a carpenter, to pull it down. He took the roof, all the weatherboards and all the lining, and put them on the train to Strahan. From there it came round to Stanley in a little boat, the *Taroa*, and my goodness, what a little boat. Harold took the uprights, and that was all he got for doing it.

All of Uncle Jack's house came round too. Uncle Jack's house here was built out of their cowshed at Strahan. That cowshed was nearly as big as a hall. It had a seat all along one side, about a foot wide. And it had beautiful pine floors. Huon pine. They're still in the house.

When Mother had the house built here, two old fellows came from Wynyard to do it, Bray and Tatlow. Tatlows had the livery stables in Smithton. The stables are still there, where we used to put our horses. They had the coach run through for Burnie and at one stage I think they drove the coach from Queenstown to Gormanston.

Father took Bob out of school at Zeehan when he was twelve and brought him round to Scotchtown away from Mother. It was an awful thing to do. She didn't want to come to Scotchtown. She went to Strahan and stayed a while with her parents after the family left. But she came afterwards when she couldn't stand being so far away from them.

We brought our cows round from Zeehan. We had two or three heifers and a couple of very good cows. One was called Myrtle, a big roan heifer, about two years old. They just used to roam the country at Zeehan. Then one day we found her shut in a paddock up past the old Railway Hotel. It was real cattle duffing.

My brother Bob came home and said, 'Mother, Myrtle is shut up in a paddock with a wire fence'. When Mother and Bob went there, they saw these men and said it was her heifer. One said he was quite sure it wasn't. It was his. But Mother had a good tongue if she wanted to tell somebody off, so Bob got Myrtle out and brought her home. And we kept a watch on her. When my father came he put the cattle on the train in Zeehan to go to Burnie. These two fellows were on the station and my father was standing watching them. And if you only knew how my father could glower at anybody! They knew he had them bluffed and they never said a word. Anyway, my father drove the cattle through from Burnie to Uncle Will's at Mount Hicks and he bought a few more at a sale at Yolla and drove them all through to Scotchtown.

Father was sick, I'll give him that, but we were so frightened of him. And he didn't know anything about farming. But he was very honest and he couldn't bear anybody to tell a lie. He built a cowshed and he was no carpenter. He stripped some bark off the trees for a roof and made the floor with hand-split timber slabs. He didn't adze them flat, so they were all peaked one after the other and you couldn't clear it out very well.

The heifers Father had just bought were supposed to be gentle but they were savages. And I was only fifteen and I couldn't milk much. So Bob and I found two old bits of rope and we made leg ropes, to tie the legs back while we were milking. But when we'd see my father coming we take them off and hide them, because we weren't supposed to have them.

We had a pig. She had a snout that long. I've never seen a pig with a snout like hers. She had young in a hollow log way down at the back of the farm. And to get her home my father sent Bob and me to carry them back in a milk dish. It was easily three feet wide and six inches deep with sloping sides and a flat bottom, moulded in one piece. You set the milk in it and skimmed it because there were no separators.

We had to chase the sow off and I had to keep her away while Bob crawled into the log. It was a terrible long way in and the sow never took any notice of me. I hit her snout with a bit of paling, but she never took a bit of notice. Here was Bob in there with the pig coming in behind. I was terrified and I thought she'd be killing him. He kicked and kicked and the pig squealed and squealed. There was this terrible scrummage and I was outside terrified to move. I expected to see his legs chewed up because pigs are very savage and you can't hurt them

Scotchtown

by hitting them. Well, eventually Bob came out and if you heard him call me names! I don't blame him.

We got her out and drove her down to River Bend in the opposite direction from home, right down to the bottom of the hill. Then Bob reckoned he could get back and get the piglets into the dish. Well, we did. There was nine little pigs. And then we couldn't find the sow. The old pig was knocked out. So we had to put the dish down and stir the little pigs up with a stick to make them squeal till the sow'd come. And she'd open her mouth as wide as a barn door and run at us if she saw us. All the way up the hill we had to keep putting the dish down and stirring up the pigs to get the old sow chasing us home.

Father lost the first property to the bank. And the people who bought it wanted to come in. We had to move and my father was just about dying. In fact he was too sick for us to shift him. I wasn't home then, I was up at Moina. There was an old house that had been somebody's first when they came into the district. There were walls and a fireplace and a few slabs on the floor. But it was just an old tumbledown shed and Mother said, 'I'm not going to live in that. I'm not', she said. 'I couldn't.'

So Pearl said, 'You don't have to'. She struck the match that burnt it down. Bob knew all about it. He told me when I came home. But Father never knew anything about it. A little while after, he died. He was getting the timber to build the place at Trowutta, but he died. He was buried in the Scotchtown cemetery. The people at Irishtown were very hurt that he wasn't buried there. We stayed with the Sawleys then. My sister Syl was married to Ted Sawley.

There was a lot of work on the roads, because they were all being made – a couple of miles one year and a mile or so the next. First of all they'd clear and grub the roots up. All you'd have was a dirt track and that's where the road would go. By the time they'd put the road in perhaps they'd alter the direction a bit, cut a corner off. The first roads were a lot longer, a lot more bends and corners than there would be when they were made later. And a lot of the road was corduroy, split cords. In the very early days they used mainly bullocks over those.

shoe last

Father had a contract to build the section of road south of Scotchtown towards Irishtown. It got the name Snottynose Road. We had a blacksmith's bellows and a very big anvil to sharpen the picks. He used to get bags of charcoal and do quite a bit himself. Most people had an anvil. We had a last to mend the shoes on, too. Father was already so ill by then he could scarcely sit on his horse to oversee the men. He used to lie by the side of the road. His horse Melba would crop the grass. She would never leave him. Originally the stone for road metal was all hand knapped. But Father had a stone crusher. The big heaps of stone on the side of the road were stacked as square as a brick, waiting for the crusher.

The summer of 1914 was terrible. Fires raged from one end of Trowutta to the other. There were blackened trees all around. My father was putting the road in, and when they saw the fire coming all the men but one pulled the stones out of the middle and buried themselves in the heap. But one poor old fellow, a Mr Williamson, he ran across the road and was burnt to death. On the morning of the very bad fire, Colin was at Roger River and it took him most of the day to get back. There was a lot of scrub, 500 acres in one lot, and that caught alight. The fires seemed to start up everywhere that day and burned all along the road. He got to our place at half past twelve at night and you never saw such a sight. When he knocked and I opened the door he was like a ghost and his clothes were black. And he'd had so much smoke. He'd gone through the fires and his hat caught alight several times.

The fires had burnt all in and he was travelling over the burnt country where the fires had been all day. He said he was worried about us. We gave him a meal and a bath and got him into bed. Then Colin went straight back out to those farms. There was a terrible lot of stock lost. And cows had their udders burnt. About a week later they took all the cattle away down and put them on the coast runs, to keep them until the country recovered.

That was the worst fire ever. At Ryans' Mrs Ryan was burnt to death and the two children were the only things left alive on the farm. The children and a cat. The little boy got the girl down and laid on top of her and put the sparks out. The mother fell over a burning stake and she was all burnt. They said it was terrible to look at the expression on her face. They only had two children. The girl went into a convent later and died very young.

There was a lot of work scrub cutting. All the men had a good sharp axe. They used to go out felling timber, splitting posts and splitting pickets, and cutting wood. So it was very important that their axes were razor sharp.

Arthur Crole sliced his stomach open with an axe once. Right from under the ribs. He was only fairly young and he just dropped it. They would have had to take him twenty miles to the doctor in Smithton. The roads were bad so they sewed him up on the spot with a hair out of a bullock's tail. It was supposed to have been sterilised. Harry Butler was very careful about that. Arthur never even went to the doctor and it just got all right. The axe wouldn't have been dirty.

Trees were very big. They used to put a shoe in, that was a solid timber slab to stand on, and climb up to cut them down. They'd put a face in one side They used to cut as they went in the green bark and put the shoe in and stand up. Then they'd have to put another one to climb up and then they'd cut from that.

In the real early days there was no mills. They never milled any of the myrtle forest. It was all just burnt and that was the tragedy. We burnt myrtle wood for years for warmth and cooking. Firewood was all myrtle. Down in the gullies all through Edith Creek was hardwood. And the blackwoods were out towards the Arthur River. Later there were mills in different places all along the river. There was a mill way up the back of Roger River West and another out at the Arthur River at one time. Then there was another mill way back of Trowutta. Dunkley's mill was between Edith Creek and Roger River. That was burnt down. The roof fell in on the whistle and it blew for half an hour. The people at Trowutta didn't know what had happened. The Dunkleys came from Zeehan. I worked with them there, for Mrs Dunkley. They owned a lot of the mills.

There were mills everywhere. There'd be a sawmill and seven or eight houses. They'd set up and go for a few years and then that area would be cut out. Then they closed the mills and started to cart the logs into Smithton. It was after the First War when centralisation started. Instead of having all the little mills and people living on the spot, Uncle Cliff and Uncle Bob and all those fellows used to work out at the mill at the back of Trowutta.

When the railway was going the cut timber used to go away on the train. They used to bring logs from way out over the back of Trowutta. The Bishops who lived on the flat just past Roger River had teams of horses and timber wagons. Bishop's stables were on both sides of the road. Mr Bishop had a good many draught horses. There'd be four in a team and he had his drivers. They'd get one load in a day. It was a long day for them. Their teams used to bring logs down and put them on the train. There was a horse tram right down to the station. There'd be stacks of cut timber waiting to go. Mackays sent all their timber to Smithton and it went over to the mainland by boats from Smithton.

At one spot there was what they called 'the travellers' tree'. It was an apple tree hanging over a fence and the timber carters used to sit under the tree for their lunch. They'd be coming down that Trowutta Hill at night. The horses knew their way. They knew what they had to do. But it makes me go cold now to think of them coming down that hill at night, because it was so muddy and slippery.

We had a lot of storms at Trowutta. We'd have hail storms, a lot of hail, and electrical storms, thunder and lightning. Usually they weren't really serious. But George Porteus was killed, struck by lightning, working with a tractor. He was terrified of thunder and evidently he was working with a tractor in a paddock going down the Spinks Creek and it was struck by lightning. Anyhow he didn't come home from work that night. His wife was terrible disappointed because she'd cooked this special tea for her birthday. She was pretty lame. So she asked his brother to go and look for him. And the brother didn't go. They didn't find George for two days. He was supposed to deliver groceries for a man who did deliveries twice a week. And George was to do it but didn't turn up. That's when they all got worried and went looking for him. And they found him.

Those cold, sleety haily showers seem to stand out because there seemed to be so much of that kind of weather. But we were never afraid of thunder or lightning. The kids would say, 'That was Santa Claus rolling his boxes', and we'd stand at the window watching the lightning. We didn't take any notice. And if the garden couldn't stand a joke, it just had to get on the same as we did.

We got a lot of wind that'd blow the trees down. In the early days they had pack horses with big saddles with hooks on them, and they used to pack the bread and the meat and things and hang so many bags on each side of the horse. A fellow had two pack horses laden with goods for Trowutta and in this terrible storm a tree fell. It hit the horse he was riding on the nose but didn't kill it and he was sitting there on the horse in the middle of the tree and the pack horses were behind him on the other side of the tree.

Later when we got the telephone at Trowutta it was a common thing for trees to come down over the line. It doesn't rain nearly as much as it used to. Once the forest is cleared you don't get nearly so much rain. Where there's trees it always rains. It was as cold as cold.

But we didn't get the heavy frosts we'd have at Zeehan. At Zeehan we'd have ten or twelve frosts in a row and in the shade it wouldn't thaw, but the days were beautiful. The days were seldom so nice at Trowutta. There was always a wind. Snow lay on the ground once in Trowutta. Between our house and the barn it was seven inches deep. But I saw snow nearly two feet deep at Moina.

Up in Trowutta there were never any floods. A culvert might be washed away, but the Spinks Creek, if it was up to the bottom of the bridge that would be very high. The kids came home from school one day and said the water was just over the bridge at Spinks Creek. And I said, 'If that's the case you're not going to school tomorrow'. But then they had to own up that it wasn't, it was only to the bottom. The river used to rise very high. Sometimes it came over the road, but it wasn't very bad. It used to be bad down at Roger River. That would flood over the paddocks. The houses were never in danger but it used to lap the shop steps. They caught a blackfish in the backyard of one place.

Ruby with Mary's son, Peter Morice

There was one big flood. That was in 1929. A woman was having a baby and she just got over the river before the flood. Phyllis was staying with us and it rained all night and all day and all night again and part of the next day. Every house in Trowutta leaked. We had to move all the furniture, pull it away from the outside walls and put it against the inside walls. The kitchen walls were all wet. You could have pulled all the paper off. It was the only time it ever happened. We had to put the beds wherever it was dry. Our son Col was only a baby and I put a big rug in the bath we used to scald the pigs and put him in that in the middle of the floor. I've never seen a night so dark and black. I had a line full of nappies and I said, 'I'm going out to bring those napkins in'. And I couldn't even see to go across the yard.

When you came to the back door at the top end of Trowutta where we lived later, those hills out over the back were the most glorious blue. That's the real truth. I remember a dull sort of misty rainy day, cold and not very pleasant, but there were wattles all coming out through the gum trees. It was really very beautiful and all the drips on the wet leaves – if there came a little bit of sun they'd sparkle.

I remember Mary Morice, who helped me in the Post Office, looking through the kitchen window one morning. It was a frosty sort of day and she said, 'Oh, I'd like to fly away to the hills!' And I said, 'Yes, and you'd pretty soon be glad to come back and sit by my stove and ask me for a hot scone!'

anvil

Chapter 7

Trowutta

"All this country was under bush and ferns ... The timber was so thick you couldn't get your fingers between the trees."

Ruby

We went back to Trowutta after our honeymoon because we had nowhere to live. I was home for a couple of months and we never had a penny to bless ourselves with. We were only just married when one of Colin's cousins was very sick. And my husband left his job at Kay's store in Irishtown and went to look after him and his wife and baby till he died. We never thought anything of that.

Then we went onto a farm. It's a light red soil at Trowutta, with lots of mudstone. All this country was under bush and ferns. Trowutta is a plateau and it was all myrtle country. They were beautiful myrtles with a real pink touch. Anywhere there was deep bush you'd find man ferns. With all the fresh fronds showing they were lovely. Down round Nabageena and Edith Creek was all stringy-bark. There were odd blackwoods at Trowutta, but it wasn't noted for blackwoods. They were down on the flats. There was a lot at Roger River and out towards the Arthur River. The mountain laurel was just beautiful and on the edges of the plain was where the waratah grew.

myrtle

Col bought the land from his cousin Dave McDonald. But he had to clear it and build the house. And the timber was so thick you couldn't get your fingers between the trees. The first house we had was up Trowutta Hill and Mopoke Gully. It was a very lonely place. There wasn't a house anywhere near us and I was a bit frightened. There were great big trees at the back and I used to say they were sighing of a night. We cut them down and had them made into shingles. They were gums, hard wood, and they made the best shingles. There was still one there when we left.

blackwood

When there were only a few people and before any telephone in Trowutta there was this big old hollow gum tree. It was called 'the post office tree'. Everybody that went into Smithton and Irishtown – most people bought all their goods in Irishtown – they used this big hollow tree as a post office. If they rode in they'd bring out all the mail, or if they could carry anything, they would. Anybody that wanted anything, they'd come along and put perhaps a five-pound note and a list under a stone, and whoever was going in would take the money and bring the things back and put the stone on the change. Nobody ever lost even a threepenny bit.

It depended on the time of year how long it took to get into Irishtown. The mud would be so thick you'd have to lift your feet in the wintertime. Where the horse's feet went there'd be deep holes until they got a few cartloads of earth and stones to ram it down. Then it'd be dry and crusty on top and wet underneath, very heavy going. On a good day the fifteen miles to Irishtown would take you three hours. If you were a man and you could trot or gallop you could get in pretty quick. Sometimes I carried Frank Sawley, my sister Syl's boy, out here in front of me on a horse, when he was a little fellow. We'd walk the horse all the way from Scotchtown and I'd carry him. And my word, I used to be stiff and sore when I got to Trowutta.

When we got a road, you'd always leave fairly early in the morning. Then you'd be coming home in the dark. This was years later when we used to go to Smithton. We'd take our horse and put it in Tatlow's livery stables. They'd take the horse out of your jinker or buggy and they'd feed it for about eighteenpence for the day. And you'd get it when you were ready to go home. That was always pretty late. We used to go to the Coffee Palace sometimes and have our dinner. That cost a shilling.

The house Col built had two rooms and a ten-foot verandah on the front, which was great. It never had a skillion, but when Madge was twelve months old we closed in one end of the verandah because Colin's father and mother were coming to stay. We never had a back porch. I made steps at the back door. We put the dairy against one end.

Flies – you've never seen flies like them! They were March flies, about February we'd have these. They were like bees, you wouldn't believe it unless you saw it. They were so thick that it'd take you all your time to get a sup of tea. When I'd pour it we'd all put our saucer on top of our cup and take it off to have a drink. And you'd still find a drowned fly. And Col's

Grandfather and Grandma Paul

mother said, 'Well, people won't believe me, but it'll be something to tell them when I go home, about the March flies'.

She'd be sitting on the verandah. She was a great one for mending. She'd do all the mending. Everywhere she'd have a needle and a thimble and she used to mend all the white embroidered nighties and camisoles and doileys. But she was the worst patcher ever I saw, because she didn't care what coloured patch she put on so long as she covered the hole. Colin thought she was a great mender and I said, 'Well, if he likes to wear her patches, good on him'.

Beautiful fancy work she did, beautiful, she never was idle. She made a white linen quilt for the first boy that got married and he beat us by about a year. We were married pretty quick after that, but I never got one. She'd always have a bit of embroidery in her pocket. And she'd pick out this bit, whatever she was doing, and she'd be sewing away.

She was fifteen when she married and she had fifteen children. Her father was a Scottish laird. His name was Masterton and the family lived at Beechworth in Victoria. They had six little girls and Colin's mother was one. Very, very staunch Presbyterians they were, very strict. On a Sunday they weren't allowed to whistle or anything like that. When she came down to Buffalo Creek to be married to Col's father they wouldn't even let her go to the gate with her husband-to-be to say goodnight to him.

Her father and another man used to buy gold from the miners and they were robbed of all this gold, and he owed so much to them. He always thought that his mate was mixed up in it, so he paid up all the miners and never had a penny left. He went up back beyond Myrtleford, to a place called Dandongadale, on Buffalo Creek.

They had a wonderful library. Her father had a whole room full of books. Their mother educated them and there was nothing Granny Paul didn't know in the way of books. Very fond of birds, she was. She studied the birds. She'd go out into the yard and be looking at all these birds. She had bird books and she knew every bird in the English language. I was staying there once and she said, 'If you just come out the back, I can show you seventeen different kinds of birds'.

Granny Paul's house at Buffalo Creek had a dirt floor and the windows had no glass, just shutters and a blind they could roll up. It was a decent enough house, two rooms and a skillion. And there was always a hut at the back that they used for a kitchen. All those early places – the husband would build the hut and live in it while he did something about the house. But they all seemed to have the kitchen like that – an old hut, quite a big room. And it was always apart from the house. Cut down a bit of heat in the summer from cooking, and fire risks.

They had it lovely about the old house with a framework built from the house covered in grapevines. And there'd be all these bunches of grapes hanging down along the verandah. The place where she washed was out in the open. It had a roof, but that was all. It had a big bench and a copper and stand, big round tubs and big round dress baskets. It was 'all among gum trees'. They sing that on TV these days. Well, she had all that.

I didn't wear a sun bonnet, like Mother used to when she was out in the garden or getting the firewood or the cows. Made out of muslin the bonnets were, with two or three frills and always a frill from the neck down to protect the neck. Grandma Paul was horrified that I didn't wear one and she said, 'Ruby, you've got a beautiful complexion and you're going out in the sun spoiling it'.

At Trowutta we used to wash in kerosene cans. We had a five foot fireplace and two big iron cranes. You couldn't get bricks. The chimney was just galvanised iron. Some chimneys had plain iron, but this one didn't. It was corrugated, with wood nailed up to make stays. Not very safe, but we seemed to get by. The hearth was so many big flat stones. Two camp ovens I had for baking bread and scones and everything – but we were young and we didn't take any notice. We never had any linos for the floors, not at that stage. Just an old potato bag at the door for people to wipe their feet on.

The first ticks for the kids' beds I made out of cut-up rags. I had a kapok tick for Madge's cot and then I made this single bed one out of cut-up rags. They used to get very lumpy.

The first dinner set I had when I was married was white, all white with a fancy edge. We used to put Madge in the cot while I'd go to milk, and if it was very cold we'd bring it out into the kitchen. It used to fit through the door. One day she pulled the table cloth off through the bars of her cot and broke every piece of china! Later Madge used to play behind the chimney. She had her toys on parts of the frame. They were broken pieces of crockery, all lined up. She used to call them her 'chinas'.

One night there was a terrible storm and Cissy McDonald, Dave's widow, had her aunt and daughter coming from Irishtown to stay. When the storm came on they just had to come in. They couldn't go home because the road was so bad. And a couple of men turned up as well. We only had two rooms. There was Madge's big cot, so Mrs McPhee and the little girl had that. I slept with Madge on a stretcher in the kitchen. And the men got into my bed with Col. One old fellow, Mr Brooks, said, 'Well, I like to get into bed first. And if I've got to sleep with two other men, I hook the blankets round me and they can pull as much as they like'.

It didn't matter. You'd make do somehow if anybody came, and we used to have bad storms in those times. As the land was cleared we didn't have as much rain.

There was an old fellow who used to go off his head sometimes. He was a very polite, well-educated man. He'd been a policeman and was belted up in Melbourne and pensioned off, and every so often the pressure on his brain would cause these turns. He had a big long whip and he was flicking it and I'm sure he was seeing how close he could get without hitting me. My word, I was frightened of him. He had this silly grin on him all the time and he was talking quite nice and polite, 'Where's your husband?'

I said, 'Well, he's not home at the moment'. We had a dog called Old Sailor and he wasn't a nice dog at all, but if anyone came near Madge's pram he'd bare his teeth at them. Old Sailor came and showed he didn't like the whip, so the old fellow just walked away quite nicely.

An old Indian hawker came one day, when Cissy MacDonald was with me. I didn't have much money in the house. You just didn't. I

Madge, Lilian and Heather, c. 1921–22

had a few shillings so I bought a tea towel and said, 'I'm sorry, that's all the money I've got. I can't buy anything else'. Then he went and took his horse out of its harness and tied it to the fence and said, 'Well, I may as well have a cup of tea while I'm here'. And Cis said to me, 'If you let him come in here, I'm going home'.

So I said, 'Well, I don't give cups of tea, but a friend of mine further on at the post office does'. I was that scared, and he went away muttering. If I'd been by myself I suppose I'd have given it to him, because I'd never refuse anybody a cup of tea. But I didn't like the look of him. He might have been a bit crabby, but I don't suppose he would have done me any harm. There were several hawkers. One called Sam Ali used to stay at our place.

There was an accident once on Trowutta Hill with a timber wagon. I saw all these men running and jumping over my fence and throwing jacks and things ahead of them and I wondered what had happened. The logs used to be fastened on with chains and the chains slipped and the log rolled on the man and crushed him. I was always thankful that none of my family were timber workers.

Heather was born two years after Madge, in 1919. When we moved down to Roger River, where Colin was managing Professor Mackay's farm and his Jersey herd, we lived for two years in 'the red house'. Heather didn't want to go. She didn't like 'that old red arse'. Lilian was born while we lived there. At Roger River Heather went missing once, Heather was a big kid and she used to get very tired. This lovely sunny morning it was just about dinnertime, and Col was coming up the track with these great big bullocks with huge curving horns. And Heather wasn't about. We couldn't find her.

We looked everywhere, we ran here and there and everywhere. I was frantic. We called and called and we couldn't find her. Then I found her in the trough where the bullocks would be fed. Heather had her arm clasped round the biscuit tin. She'd gone there and was sitting in the sun having a biscuit and she'd dropped off to sleep! Lucky we hadn't called out a search party.

Professor Mackay had come through the district in a jinker with his wife, looking at the land. He was a big man, a terrible big man, never had an ounce of over-flesh on him. Mrs Mackay had very golden red curly hair, a very pretty woman and very pleasant.

Professor Mackay started a Jersey herd and used to show his cattle at the show. Because Col was the manager he had to take them and lead them. He had a prize bull named Pasha of Ban Ewell, and he didn't have a very nice nature, that bull. So Col always used to keep the ring in his nose and lead him on a chain. He reckoned that way he could handle him. And he always carried a cane when he led the bull.

Professor Mackay owned two sawmills. All the blackwood used in Parliament House in Canberra came from Mackay's mill at Roger River. He had a lot of men and horses working for him. Mr Eaves was the sawmiller and his sons worked there too. Mr Eaves wouldn't join the union and his brother-in-law Tom Hancock said, 'If God came down from Heaven and asked you to join it, I still don't think you'd join'. And Mr Eaves said, 'In the first place there ain't no such person'.

There were two shops at Roger River, Gherke's and Winser's. I never used to get anything at Gherke's. He was German and his wife was a delicate, coy little thing. I went to buy flour one day and two mice hopped out of the bag. I said, 'I don't think I'll bother with the flour now'. 'Oh,' she said, 'I haven't seen any mice'. We had no flour, but I didn't take it. I think the poor little woman thought it very bad. But I bought something else instead.

Heather was about three when we moved to the top end of Trowutta. I went back later to clean the house out and burned a lot of rubbish. Madge had a rag doll which she called Tilly and while we were away the rats had made a nest in it. So I had to burn it with this other rubbish. Tilly was just so much part of Madge's life, it was a terrible thing to have to burn that doll. She never felt the same about any other.

jersey bull

Chapter 8

The top end

"The land was covered with myrtle logs and snakes."

Like his father-in-law, Charles Pacey, whom he would scarcely have known, Colin Paul liked to be his own boss. So in 1922 after two years at Roger River, the family moved back to Trowutta to a farm called Nesdale at 'the top end'. For Ruby and her daughters this was a big advantage. To see her mother and sisters at Trowutta while she was living at 'the red house' Ruby had to walk six miles with Heather in the pram and toddler Madge walking or carried on her shoulder. With the advent of baby Lilian it became even more difficult.

At Nesdale Ruby was living much nearer. Her older sister, Syl, married to Ted Sawley, lived on the farm next door. Her younger sister Pearl, who had married Cliff Frost, the son of the postmistress, had built near the hall opposite the showground. As a wedding present Colin had given them enough shingles to roof their new house. Ruby's mother, with Grandma and Grandfather Porteus, were a little further on near the post office.

Ruby

From our place we could see Syl when she came out. She'd cooee, and we would hear her from the house. Syl was real ladylike. A lot of people called her 'the duchess'. But my word, she was good to the kids. She'd take all of them and they'd go for a picnic. If they only had bread and jam, it'd be a picnic. But if the boys were teasing the girls sometimes, she'd say 'The only thing with a spout we'll take to the picnic is a teapot' and she'd only take the little girls!

Syl used to take the girls straight down towards the gully – that's the Roger River – it comes right through the gully. They'd go there to catch beautiful lobsters and blackfish. And they'd just take some bread and the frypan and knew they'd get enought fish for their dinner. They'd cook it over an open fire with this old black frypan.

The cousins are still very close because they grew up so close and had so much to do with each other. They were a bit clanny in those days. Another family lived up there and the kids used to go and hide up the hill among all the black myrtle logs and stones and bush in case those others caught up with them. They were sufficient unto themselves.

There was a piece of land on a corner of Brydges Road reserved by Canon Brydges for a Church of England. But it was never built. He held the first Anglican church service in the open air by a big log and the log was there for years. Pearl and Syl were at that service, but I wasn't here then. The first service I ever remember was up at the school. It was used for church services until the hall was built. Nearly everybody went to whatever service was being held, whether it was Methodist, Presbyterian or whatever. We went, it didn't matter what they were. But the Catholics nearly always went to Irishtown. Church was a very important part of the community.

Madge was christened in the school, and Heather too. One day Madge got her fingers in the inkwell. I had nothing to wipe her hands with, so I took off her lacy bonnet and used that. Mrs Dunstan was playing the little old organ that Mrs Crole used to bring and she got the giggles. She was a terror to laugh.

I remember Pearl sent young Cliff to church one morning and for some reason she didn't go with him. When he came home she said, 'Well, what did you learn in church?' And he said, 'There was a fellow there talking about a poley goat'. His mother explained about the Holy Ghost. But he was only a little boy and that night when his father was going out to milk he had his old milking clothes on, this terrible old pullover. And Cliff said, 'Mum, I think Dad is the Holy Ghost'.

There was always a clear patch along the fence so we used to walk along the fence line, across the paddocks coming home from church. Frank Sawley when he was a little fellow was going along and he was singing *Lord God Almighty* when he tripped on a root. He said, 'Bugger that root', and went on singing, with his hands behind his back.

There was a Presbyterian minister who used to come out sometimes, he was Scotch, a very nice man. He was holding a service in Croles' home one day. The great big open fireplace was smoking and the room was filled with smoke. So Mr Crole got up in the middle of the service and pulled the fire to pieces and carried it outside, so the minister could go on preaching.

One day Harry Butler went to sleep in church and started to snore, and the minister, Henry Jerrim, said he took one look at me and had to close the service because he had a job to say the prayers. Harry Butler's wife was Church of England and he was always taken to church. He didn't want to go, but he had to. Another day during the service he was studying this bill for some timber he'd got from Lees mill at Smithton, adding it up and checking it to see it was all right. That was another day the minister knew what was going on.

Once a lay preacher came to visit us. He was a Mr Fawkner, he came out from Stanley and helped. Pearl and I were milking Sawley's cows and she had gone into the bedroom to get her old milking clothes. In the meantime this fellow came and sat on a chair with its back to the bedroom door. She wanted me to get her boots and she was dancing the hornpipe in her bare feet behind his back. I got her boots in and first I heard one plonk and then another plonk. She'd dropped them out the window and then she followed. And there she was pulling faces through the window and there he was sitting talking to me and he didn't know what I was laughing at. I had to think of something funny to tell him. So I told him about the politicians being tipped in the mud.

Our boundary was at the foot of the hill and along Brydges Road, where the land was covered with myrtle logs and snakes. There were two big bare myrtle trees blackened by fire, that were landmarks. And there used to be a stump on the corner that looked like a policeman bending. There was grass but there were logs all the way across it and Col would clear it and put in a paddock of swedes. Then perhaps he'd put potatoes in that paddock. There's a beautiful spring right in the back corner of the block and there was always plenty of water. The kids used to come home from school and walk right down near the spring and away over to the other corner to get the cows. They'd bring the cows home through these logs and there were some big snakes down there.

There was a thicket of trees and a little creek. The creek was a good place to wash the men's trousers, because they'd be pretty muddy. A few people had windmills, but not very often. It was mostly a windlass and a bucket and a rope. Syl's well was eighty feet deep, one of the deepest in Trowutta. Mostly they struck water long before that. But hers was right on top of a hill and they were going to deepen it.

A man was going down and the rope broke and he went right to the bottom. He broke both his legs and that's all that happened to him. There was an old Irishman, Connie Brouder, at the top where they had just let him down and he got down on his knees and looked over the edge and called down the well, 'Micky, Micky, tell me, Micky, are you killed?'

Tasmanian tigers were never a trouble. We called them hyenas. They said there was one came out onto these paddocks in the early days and killed a baby lamb. They said they used to kill the sheep so they were killed out. But they never did any damage here, and there were a lot of them. They were very shy animals. They won't touch you, but they'll follow you for miles, sort of track you. There was one captured here and taken to old Mr Harrison's zoo in Wynyard, but that's the only one I ever saw. Croles had a rug made from the skin of a hyena caught in a trap. They had it over the back of a chair.

Heather and her husband Murray thought they saw one in the 1940s. They were coming home from a ball and were so sure they'd seen it when they came round the corner with the car lights on, that Murray came out again next day and went away up into the bush to try to track it. They were so shy that you'd only get a fleeting glimpse of them anyway. But there's miles and miles of bush out here and it's not very far through to the plains where they would get any amount of food, young wallabies.

But the Tasmanian devils were very destructive. They'd clean up a poultry yard in a night. Murray used to ride a bike up here before he and Heather were married. One Sunday night riding home a Tasmanian devil followed, snapping at the pedals as they went round.

Then there were the wombats, we called them badgers. And the tiger cat and the native cat. And wallabies and kangaroos of course. The men went snaring in the wintertime. We made kangaroo tail soup and wallaby patties. I used to love a wallaby, a young wallaby. I'd like

The top end

one now. But there were no rabbits until the railway line came soon after the end of World War One. One night Col was coming home through Edith Creek and his dog caught one. He said he knew nobody would believe him, so he tied the pelt up to the ceiling in the kitchen to prove that he'd seen this rabbit.

As soon as the bush was cleared the starlings and sparrows came. I don't remember blackbirds until a lot later. There were black cockatoos. But the white cockatoos didn't come until later when the land was cleared. They didn't come very often but they were a menace when they did. They came when we were putting the crops in. Later there were magpies in the big pear tree at the back of the post office. Out the back of Gran's place there was a pair of magpies. One year I remember four or five. We were always excited when we saw the magpies because they only came sometimes. They seem to have gone now.

The Pacey sisters. L–R: Sylvia Sawley, Ruby Paul, Pearl Frost, Emily (Phyllis) Hancock

Ruby of Trowutta

thylacine

Chapter 9

Colin Paul

"Colin wasn't one to talk about his achievements, but he reckoned he was the only schoolboy that ever caught W.G. Grace out!"

Ruby

On Sunday morning, even right up until Col was sick, he used to go out with the gun and he'd take five cartridges with him. But he never came near the house with his gun loaded, and you'd see him unload his gun as he came along way out the other side of the cowshed. He'd go out with five cartridges and he'd come home with five hares.

I never ever knew him to come home with less hares than cartridges. If he brought home three, he'd have two cartridges left. And he never hit one in the behind. He wouldn't shoot at them if they were running away. They were always shot in the head. I never thought anything of it until years later, and I thought then, 'Well, he must've been a wonderful shot'. Hares were part of our staple diet in those days.

Jack Harris – he was a carpenter who built most of the early places in Trowutta – he would come to tea and he'd say, 'Make me a hare pie, Missus, make me a hare pie'. I used to cook the hare with some bacon all day in the old Peters oven, and over the top of it I used to put seasoning, then let it all brown.

But once the rabbits came the hares practically disappeared.

Col was really marvellous with dogs. He never spoke to a dog. He used to whistle him. They used to want him to train dogs, and he said well, nobody else could work his dogs because he never spoke to them. But when they did the right thing, he'd always give them a good pat and say, 'Good fellow'. That's all he ever did. He had a particular whistle for everything. He'd whistle a dog to sit down. The dog would sit down and if he didn't tell him to come, that dog would still be there in a couple of hours, waiting until he got the whistle to 'come on'.

He had one that he called Jim and he really was a most marvellous dog. He was a big black sleek dog with a little white and tan on his face. In later years when Col was driving the cattle from Smithton he used to go in the car and the dog would go ahead along any side roads so that the cattle wouldn't go off the road or into anybody's paddock. Sometimes it'd be quite dark when they got home and you could always depend on Jim bringing all the cattle home.

One night Col called in at the post office to get the mail and when he came out, the dog was gone. The dogs used to ride on the side of the car, but they were never allowed inside. He called him and he whistled him. But he couldn't find him anywhere. He drove home and still called and whistled and he never came. They'd been out droving all day and Dad thought, 'All right, I'll have to go back and look for him tomorrow'.

But when he pulled up in his own garage, the dog sat up off the back seat. He'd been so tired that he'd been asleep and he never heard Dad calling him. And Col said, 'I forgot to scold him for being on the back seat of the car. I was just so pleased to see him'.

One dog we had was Hempy. He was a beautiful dog with long hair and a white ruffle round his neck. Col's people had a Hempy in Myrtleford when he was a boy, so he called this dog after him. The kiddies used to saddle him up, harness him up in a coach. They were allowed to play with Hempy. They used to put string around his neck and ride him. But they were never allowed to play with Jim, because Dad reckoned they'd spoil him. Even as they got a bit older they were never allowed to take Jim off the chain to go even for the cows, to make him work.

We had three paddocks and big herds of cows and we herded them with the dogs. We had another dog called Bob and they were allowed to take him. And the cows would know if you only took him, but if you went without him they'd know too. Then you'd have to drive every one of them home. They wouldn't come. There used to be big logs and they'd get behind the logs.

Hempy would come, even though he was getting very very old, and he knew what he had to do. But they were never allowed to take the good dog, never. Col would have a dog for a little while, and if he wasn't going to be a good dog, he wouldn't bother with him. We never had a sick dog. We had good country, they were well fed and I don't think there were those diseases about. It was only rarely you would hear of somebody's dog getting sick.

There were very few sheep in Trowutta, but we always had some. We never kept them long as a rule. We'd only buy perhaps a hundred and keep them for a little while. Col used to do a lot of dealing, to buy and sell a lot of cattle in the paddock. He worked for the auctioneer, Farmers and Graziers. When we had sheep we used to get a shearer in. It was all done by hand, by blade.

Col's family came out on the *Schomberg* which was wrecked in 1855 off Portland in Victoria. There were three brothers, Sam, Joe and Jim, who came out from Scotland and they took up land around Myrtleford. They all had very big families and they're all over Australia now. A lot of them went to Queensland and some are about Melbourne.

Colin really would have been a very clever man if he'd had an education. The schoolmaster wanted his father to send him away to be a doctor, but it was very expensive. The schoolmaster offered to pay half if the father could find the other half. But his father couldn't even affford half, with all the other children in the family. His father wasn't an educated man, but he built the school to have his children educated.

A very strict Presbyterian was Col. He never had a drink of anything stronger than tea or water until just before he died. Then the doctor recommended stout and it just about broke his heart. The doctor wanted to give him a glass of beer before a meal. So everybody that came used to bring him a bottle of beer and his locker at the hospital was full of beer. The sister thought he was a drunkard. But he never drank it.

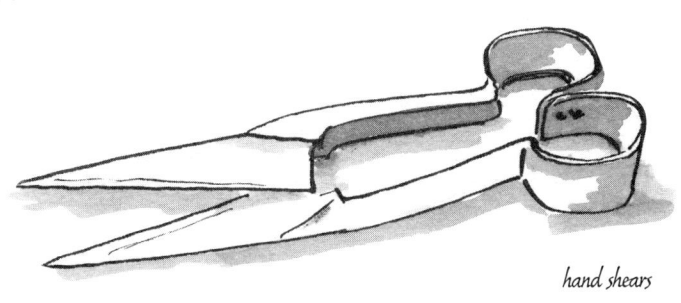

hand shears

Colin Paul with son Colin and dog Bob

He had immaculate manners. He'd be very cross with me for saying that. But he was very strict. Arthur Ambrose was from Scotland and he got a chain of stores eventually. But he was just fourteen and in short trousers when he first came to our place in Trowutta. Three lads used to come round in a big bus, and they used to carry drapery, everything you could imagine on this bus. Two of them used to sleep in the house and one used to sleep in the bus with the revolver. They had a bed right up in the roof.

And later when they came to the post office Colin was very cross because I called him Arthur instead of Mr Ambrose! And he'd been coming since he was fourteen and in short trousers! He would never tolerate Christian names at all.

He was very careful. I was always in hospital for all my babies. He always thought your wife ought to be where she'd get attention when she wanted it. That's one thing he always said. Pearl never went till she had to and she just had to take a chance over the roads. But Colin wasn't like that. I went early and sometimes I was there two or three weeks before. I was warned once by a doctor who stood by my bed, 'Never let anybody let you out of bed under three weeks'. But I didn't want a rest.

Auntie Phyllis looked after the children or Colin looked after them himself. He used to roast a leg of lamb and he'd roast big lumps of swede and potatoes. He used to make stews and great big pots of soup. And huge pots of potato.

Once he took Madge into Irishtown and he had two sides of bacon he had cured. And he sold them to Kay's store and he brought home three coats for the price he'd got for the bacon. That's how we used to live in those days in Trowutta. And he bought those terribly expensive hats at Kay's in Irishtown, that cost about ten times as much as the ones we made. Yet he would never let us waste a thing. He was the most honest man.

He was a big man, about six foot three, very muscley and active, and terribly, terribly fond of sport, all sorts of sport, but mainly cricket. The Pauls had a cricket team, all Pauls from Colin's own family and a couple of cousins. They'd always have a game of cricket on Sunday afternoon after church. Colin wasn't one to talk about any of his achievements but he reckoned he was the only schoolboy that ever caught W.G. Grace out. And he was only thirteen!

The captain had put Dad at silly point, just out from the bat, and W.G. Grace said, 'I wouldn't stand there if I were you, sonny'. And Col said, 'My captain said so'.

And W.G. Grace said, 'Look out, boy, I'll put it through you'.

Col said, 'I was determined to stand my ground. And I got it straight at me. I couldn't believe my eyes. I doubled over it'. It hit him in the stomach. And he caught it.

They still talk about it up at Myrtleford. It was in Country Week Cricket at Wangaratta. He didn't tell us very much. But that was one story Col used to tell us.

Col was never one to talk about his achievements. But at the Irishtown football ground he was playing cricket there one day – and he put one straight over the top of the station which was out the other side. The train yard and track were directly behind the grandstand and the station and platform were beyond. And Dad put one clean over the top. He said he heard a little boy afterwards say, 'Gee, they wouldn't have done much good today, if it hadn't been for that Colin Paul'.

As he got older and he wasn't very well he still played cricket. He'd go out and take his turn with the bat and had a runner. He still played until he couldn't hold the bat, and then he was umpiring for a long time.

He was very fond of natural things. I remember him coming home from shooting expeditions with a little sprig of wild violets. Tiny little things they were, and he'd put them in the band of his hat to carry them. Or he'd come home with some interesting little bit of foliage.

But if he ever found a white daisy, not the tiny ones that are in lawns, but the bigger ones that stand up, he'd bring those home and burn them, because they become a weed and a pest in the pastures. There was a patch used to grow down our boundary fence and he'd go along every year. He'd go for a

wild violets

walk on a Sunday morning and he'd come back with a handful of these pulled up by the roots and burn them.

He had a very strict code of ethics. He used to spend quite a bit of time with the kiddies and they did a lot of things together. But everything he did and everything he said had to be just so exact. I think that probably sums up Col so much.

When Col's mother got sick, they said she had a year to live. So Col sold all his cattle and went to stay with her for the last year of her life. And he left me with four little girls. Would people do that now? I don't think they would.

He was away the best part of a year, he didn't stay till his mother died. I wrote to him and told him he'd better come home and earn some money, and he came home at Christmas.

The Paul sisters. L–R: Madge, Heather, Lilian, Merle

Chapter 10

The farm

"The cows lived a hard life."

Ruby

When first we were farming in the Trowutta district, nobody had any more than a hundred acres, because that was all one man could manage with pick and shovel and axe. He'd clear a patch and then his tracks and his fencing were all done by hand. They didn't have any machinery.

Gradually as the land got cleared, there wasn't work for more people, and a family would go away, or if someone died, a neighbour would buy the property. He could manage two then. Later when they had tractors and bulldozers that made it easy. And cars to travel quickly from one place to another. So now there are properties of hundreds and hundreds of acres. And the herds have grown.

Col had a smudger. Everybody used to have a smudger. He always called it a smoodger. It was like an upside down sledge, because all the timber part had to be down on the ground and the two crosspieces they were nailed to stick up in the air. If you turned it over you could use it for a sledge. After the ground was worked up and the seeds were put in, it had to be smoothed over. The kids would ride on the smudger and that'd smooth the ground all out. They would want to stand up, not sit down, and Merle fell. So there she was being dragged along with her backside still on the smudger and her head coming along behind, full of dirt!

They wouldn't use a sledge on the road, they used them in the paddocks to bring things out. Sledges were made with long runners and they didn't make as much mess as wheeled vehicles, because they'd just slide over the top. Usually one horse could pull it. If you had your dray or your wagon, it was making wheel tracks along the way. So sledges were easier to use even where it was muddy. It's very heavy rainfall, so there's a lot of mud and wheeled vehicles in the wintertime just get bogged. Wheeled vehicles cost a lot more and the sledges are homemade. They weren't expensive, because they'd just make them out of the wood they had on the place. But they'd have to put them together with very strong iron spikes. Nails wouldn't be any good. They'd soon rattle to pieces with nails.

They had what they called a shoe – the fork of a tree and it's smooth – and you can harness a horse to that. And it'll pull anywhere because there's hardly anything touching the ground and it's not a great weight. They could carry any load at all, a great log, calves or cattle feed. The two branches of the fork had holes where the chains or the harness was hooked in. And they'd put a steel tyre under the runners, because the stones would wear them.

When we had horses, everybody had horses. There'd be a horse to ride and a horse for the cart. We'd grow oats, and chaffcutters would come round. There'd be about twenty or two dozen men and they would have to be fed. Nobody had freezers or fridges, of course, and it would nearly always be corned beef and carrots and things like that. All this gang would have to be fed for three or four meals, depending on how much you had to cut. Where it was grain country, they'd have them for perhaps a week or fortnight. They were fed in the kitchen, but a lot of them used to sleep in the hay or on the chaff out in the barn. People couldn't put that many men up at a time. There was a lot more oaten hay then, not so much grass hay, because the grass paddocks had not been properly cleared, so you couldn't have got through with machinery, even if you had the right sort.

You'd have about twenty-four men and they'd be there for two or three days with the chaff-cutter and the drum, that's the thrasher. They used to build haystacks. They went to a place and if they weren't treated too well they made a mess of the bathroom. At some places they did get a lean time. At one all they were given was curry gravy and the occasional sausage. They said, 'A pound of sausages doesn't go far, even curried, between all of us'. But for the main they were well treated. If you looked after them, they looked after you usually. They'd give you a fair go.

When Colin died and we had the chaffcutter come, these boys all came. They were there for two days and when they went off they

The farm

wouldn't take any money, except the owner charged just to set the engine up. Colin had played cricket with them for years and one Saturday afternoon the bus to take them home after the match broke down. So we had the whole cricket team to our place to give them tea. We made them big plates of sandwiches. So they wouldn't take a penny, not a penny.

But my word, you had to cook. For breakfast they'd have porridge and chops and fried potatoes or something sustaining. And no sooner than you'd get them out of your way than you'd have to get something ready for their morning tea. And they wouldn't wait till you went out with it. They'd blow the whistle at a certain time and you had to be there. Always a break through the morning. And that was big trays of scones and big trays of rockies. But if you didn't have something cooked up before they got there, you couldn't keep up because you just didn't have the time. Then dinner had to be right on. When they blew the whistle for dinner you had to be ready. You'd have big pie dishes a foot long. You'd make apple pies the day before and make your plum puddings, and they were real plum puddings. We didn't take any notice. We just did it.

You'd still have to milk your cows in between, because Col had to help the men and it was left to the women. Another thing that had to be got ready was a huge pile of wood, because it was all steam. Col used to cart the wood on the sledge to where they were going to set up. That would be ready a day or two before they came. But when they moved out of your paddock, lots of times you'd go on to the next to give a hand, especially if there was one woman doing it on her own.

There was the chaffcutter, the thrasher and the baler and they'd all come together with the one traction engine and set up by the stack. The sheds would all have to be ready for the chaff. The men used to carry it. They had a ladder they'd go up and tip it into a big shed Dad had lined with galvanised iron. It was good chaff.

Trowutta was a lime deficient area and the grass would only last about two or three years. At the end of five years it would all be gone. When they discovered what was wrong, then they were able to grow the clover and the grass. Nearly all oats we grew. We didn't grow wheat or barley. There might be an odd paddock but there's never really been wheat or barley grown here very much at all, not this far down the North West. Then after a few years there was the clover hay and the grass hay used to come in and that would be baled. You'd get a lot of clover and a lot of strawberry clover. And a lot of what they call cow grass, that was a clover that had a big pink strawberry-coloured flower on it. It was only very much in the latter years they made silage.

And we grew good swedes. We're noted for swedes at Trowutta. That's true. And they weren't like the swedes you buy today. There'd be any amount that'd be ten pounds each and they were just average. There was one swede twenty-eight pounds and one thirty that Col took round to Tom Brydges. He brought home this huge swede and he wanted us to scrub it up. So we got out the jam pan, but the swede was so big it wouldn't fit in, it just sat on top. When the market opened up in Sydney, the big ones were too big and they got a new strain of seed that grew smaller swedes, so you could get more in a bag. You'd just roll them into a bag. They were the most beautiful swedes.

They were lovely to eat raw, young swedes. You'd put the knife into them and they'd crack open like a carrot. You'd hear the crack when you cut them. We loved cooked swedes mashed with a teaspoon of sugar and some black pepper.

When Col was pulling swedes, which we had to do every year, his hands would crack with the mud and the cold and the wet, so he used to rub them with beeswax and tie a piece of wool around each finger that had a crack, tie the wool right into the crack, then rub over the top with beeswax. He'd warm the beeswax to get it soft, and it would keep the water out of his skin. If they were bad, I'd quite often give him a finger stall before he went to work, snagging the swedes. They used to say 'snaggin' the swedes'. They always had a sharp knife, and they'd pull with one hand, and as they pulled they'd cut the roots off. They were just so quick, you couldn't imagine the action unless you saw it. They'd grab the swede, then as they did it, they'd cut it and turn it over. They'd go right round it probably in three or four cuts and then cut the top off almost in the one movement.

We had draught horses. We always had a pair. Belle and Bloss were the main ones. Once when I was in hospital, the draught horse got stuck in the spring one Sunday morning. Nearly all the men of Trowutta were getting Pauls' horse out. They thought it was dead, but it lived. The day it happened we had swedes and potatoes and a piece of meat all cooking together in the oven in this big black dish. It was getting pretty brown by the time Col got the horse out and everybody else had gone home. Col and the kids were starving and Heather said she'd never tasted anything so nice as that baked swede.

The farm

Our track horse was Kitty. She was a nice little mare. The one we had before that was a big ginger mare Col used to call 'Old Slommick'. Minnie was her real name. There was a little ditty that he made up. All the kids right up to now, they know it. 'Old Minnie goes nim-nim-nim, Old Dolly Grey goes trit-trot, trit-trot, and the little brown foal goes gallopy, gallopy, gallopy.' Dolly had a foal, and this was our three horses when we were down at Mackay's in the old red house. We had them up in Trowutta too. Another fellow had a grudge against Dad and he shot old Dolly Grey. Shot her right through the head, in the eye. Then we had another Kitty, a pony for the children. Sawleys had one called Kitty and so did Frosts.

Gran Pacey had a horse called Calamity Jane. A big, tall, rangy chestnut she was. She was fairly fast, she had a long stride. Everybody had a horse they could put in shafts and could ride as well. Everybody had a horse and jinker. Syl had a horse called Melba after Madam Melba. She was a very well bred horse. A horse you had brought in out of the paddock you couldn't ride as fast as one that you had fed in the stable with oats and chaff. My sister Phyllis had a lot of old horses. One was Old Mac, a fairly big, tall black horse. Harry Butler had a paddock somewhere in Trowutta and that was the pound. Somebody put this horse in because it was wandering about the roads and it wasn't claimed. So Phyllis gave him ten shillings for it and when she was going off, he stuck his hand in the lapel of his coat and said, 'She were a good 'orse twenty year ago'.

Later the carters had horse teams rather than bullocks because they were faster. Charlie Bishop had teams and there would've been ten horses in them and what they called the pole, the lead horse, eleven altogether. That's how they used to take all the timber down from Trowutta to the little station which was called Trowutta but which was actually at Roger River.

Of course they needed horses for cattle mustering in the early days. They used to take them down to the coast the other side of Marrawah right down to Temma. They used to swim them across the Arthur River. The men would probably be away nearly a week when they took them and about a week again when they were rounding them up. They might have to make two or three trips to round them up. To muster them all there'd be a big lot of men that would go down and they used to bring them right up to Smithton before they'd sort them out and get their own. Everybody's cattle would be mustered together. Our brand was a P with a circle over it. My son Col's got it now.

There was a big plain out the back of Trowutta called Gibson's Plain. When they were only using a hundred acres per farm, the farms weren't big enough to have pasture all year round. So they used to take their cattle back there for the winter, get them off their paddocks after the cows were dried off and we weren't milking. They'd drive them through in a day. It would probably be a long day, but it wasn't that far, so they'd be home by night. They'd probably take them back for two months and give their paddocks a spell. Then they'd bring them home and they wouldn't be in real good order, not very fat, but they'd soon pick up. The cattle would absolutely thrive when they got into the green pastures and were hand fed again. Their coats would get smooth as anything, and they would milk.

When they'd been eating clover the milk got 'feedy'. Fresh clover or turnips. They used to feed a lot on cow turnips in the wintertime. You could put a feed out just after you milked them and they could have that. Then they'd have to be taken off half a day before you milked them, and even then you'd get a bit of a flavour. That's why we always had our night paddock to keep the cows, so that in the morning we always got our milk for the house from the first milking. The house cow was always milked first. Swedes were stronger than turnips and always flavoured the milk. There was really nothing worse. If you had that milk in your tea or on hot porridge it'd just turn you off. It turned Heather off milk forever. We never used that cream for our butter or for the house. If they had to be on that because we were short of feed, the house cow would be kept separate. We always had one cow for milk. I never ever remember our buying milk or cream.

All the cows were milked by hand. Sawleys had a milking machine and that was about the only one in the district. Sawleys' old engine used to putter away. Sometimes it wouldn't go and they had more cows than we did at that stage. Sawleys had rape for their cows too, but we didn't.

All our animals had names. Now the herds are too big and they can't have names. I suppose they number them now. But ours all had a meaning, an identity. Each cow was an individual. One family would name them all after flowers one year, and next year they'd name them all after girls. Then they'd know how old they were. We always did have a good many cows after we moved to Trowutta from Roger River.

Col always liked the milking shorthorn, Illawarra shorthorn, and he hated the little fine Jersey. Everybody was going in for Jerseys so then we had the shorthorn Jersey cross. He always liked the cattle with nice colour, the white and reds and roans. Nesdale Rose was a red cow. She got milk fever and went missing. Madge and Heather were sent to look for her. And we couldn't find her. Col went over to the neighbours to see if she had got in with their cows. This cow was sick with milk fever and she was really mad. She got up and chased Madge and Heather and they had to scramble up onto a big black log.

The roans were shorthorns. We had one called Fairy, nearly a pure Jersey, and one called Blackie, part Jersey, and they were the two most wonderful cows. We had Fairy breed, as long as we milked. And Elfie, a purebred Illawarra from up in New South Wales, used to give a bucket and a half of milk. And when I say 'a bucket', they were great big two and a half gallon buckets. Heavy tin and they'd last for years. We got Elfie from Professor Mackay, and Heather reared her from a calf out of a bucket when she was eight. She's still got the scar to prove it. Col had put up a new wire fence. Heather used to take the milk over the road to feed her and had to get over the fence. As soon as Elfie finished she'd chase Heather for the bucket, so she threw the bucket over the fence once and tore her arm open from the elbow down.

You'd have a row of buckets. We used to milk by hand and there'd be perhaps four or five of us milkers. We used to turn the buckets upside down on the fence after they were washed. You'd have to wash them or scald them. You didn't use any soap, you just washed and scrubbed them. We always had a scrubbing brush. At one stage Col's was a three-gallon bucket and all the others were two and a half. And because Heather was small she had a two gallon one. He bought it for her because she always helped with the milking, and a two and a half gallon bucket was too heavy.

Heather wasn't ever frightened of the cows. Madge was always terrified, even when they were milking after she was married and had to help. She hated the young calves and the singing out and bellowing. And Lilian was always quiet and back in the corner and she didn't seem to get into it. If Lilian even goes into the cowshed she gets hayfever. She really does. That's the truth. Merle wouldn't even learn because she was too cunning and she hated it.

We made butter once a week and it was Friday afternoon that we churned. We saved the cream from the day before. We used to put the cows on a special pasture so there'd be no feed flavour on the butter. That was a thing Col was particular about. Rank clover didn't make good butter. They'd be all right after Christmas when the clover was drying off. But you could taste the clover on the butter if you put the cows on it.

It wouldn't matter if there was a little bit of flavour for cooking. Suppose you had it off the clover paddock, you never tasted it on the cooking. When it goes to the factory they can take that taste off now, but of course they couldn't in the early days. We always had a special paddock we'd put the cows in at night and we'd always churn the morning's cream. We kept it. It was always a day old. The same morning's cream wouldn't curd like the day old. If you got cream several days old and naturally sour, that made beautiful butter. But now if you put it in the fridge it doesn't really turn sour. When it starts to go off it gets a nasty taste. It'll keep fresh in the fridge but it doesn't really turn sour like when it ripens. You're supposed to make the best butter when the cream ripens and that would be a couple of days old.

We had a dairy that had nothing else in it and it had a double wall with slats between the boards, so it got plenty of air. We always kept the cream covered and we had a special thing to stir it. We had a cream stick when we were up at the top end, but later years we had a cream stirrer. It was like a galvanised plunger – a big round disc with holes and a tall handle coming up out of the middle. We always had to make sure the cream was scraped down to the cream level, otherwise the cream'd dry and cake around the top.

The rest of the week we sent the cream to the factory. The cream bus – it wasn't really a bus, but we used to call all motor vehicles a bus in those days – used to come three days a week in the flush of the season and then it'd get to two days and then perhaps one. Later when the herds got bigger and the roads got better it came every day.

We had a little Cherry churn which churned seven pounds and a little pat at a time. That's what we'd churn every week and it was beautiful butter. We'd churn it by hand and we had a board that we called our butter board. You take it outside to the tap to wash it, wash all the buttermilk out of it. That was always saved for the pigs, and sometimes if we were a bit short of food for the pigs we'd save the first washing. The butter always had to be washed three times with clean, cold running water. The pats and the butter board and the churn was always washed first and then scalded before you started. Scalded really well with boiling water and then rinsed with cold, and your butter cloths and your pats. A lot of time we worked it by hand to wash it, and your hands were washed in hot water and then run under the cold tap. Just like the boards. And you'd cut your fingernails and clean them first always. That was the thing.

If you didn't scald the boards and run the cold tap on them the butter would stick. And you had to wring your cloth out of boiling water. Your butter cloth was sometimes an old linen tea towel, sometimes a piece of old linen that could be well scalded and run on the cold tap before you put it into the butter. It never stuck that way. You'd pat the butter all over with this cloth and you'd wring the water out, and if you didn't do it properly you'd have streaks in the butter. We'd dry it very well with this cloth because you mustn't have water bubbles on it when you cut it.

Your salt was added after the third washing and you worked your salt into it then, after you'd got it all nice and dry, all the water that you could get worked out of it. Then occasionally there'd be a little more moisture come out, but that would be probably salt. Usually the salt was worked into it and we didn't work it a lot after that until you patted it up. And you'd pat it up with the butter pats and you got so that you could get a lump of butter, pat it up and put it on the scales and you'd have the sixteen ounces. You could do it almost to a fraction. Madge has the old mould. It would make a pound of butter and put a pattern on it. You'd just push it into a lump of butter.

But we didn't have a mould until we went down to live at the post office and that was Mrs Frost's old mould. My mark on my butter was always done with the end of the butter pat and done diagonally across the butter. There was another lady who used to do hers straight across, and another used to do diagonal both ways and they'd come out in diamonds. If you sold any butter, everyone would know that that was Mrs Paul's butter, or that was Mrs Pryor's, or Mrs Sawley's. We were always allowed to sell butter, and in the wintertime if you had a surplus, you'd send it down to the shop, or you'd sell it around to anyone who didn't have any. But we nearly always had a cow in the wintertime.

We used to pot butter in the flush of the season and that always had a little bit of extra salt and a pinch of saltpetre to keep it. We had

Gran Pacey, Pearl Frost, Heather and Colin

a big butter crock, a big stoneware crock, about fifteen inches across, and eighteen inches deep, and usually the fawny stone colour with the brown top, like a lot of the crocks were in those days. They varied in size. The butter was often covered with brine and then in wintertime you'd get it out for cooking. You'd have to wash the brine off it before you used it for cooking. I didn't use it much for the table. We nearly always had a cow and we used the fresh butter.

We'd do our cooking on Saturday after the butter was made, and I always loved to start into these big pats of butter for the cooking. There was never any shortage of butter, no matter what else. But once I remember the only butter I had was on the turn. I made a fruit cake with it and everyone said it was one of the best I'd ever made! And we had our own chooks, so we had eggs. Our eggs we used to keep in waterglass. Kepeg was a thing that came later and was like vaseline. I didn't like that. But the waterglass was a solution you mixed with so much water to a bottle and you kept your eggs in that in a kerosene tin.

butter crock

If we wanted to salt a piece of meat, we used to make our own brine with salt and saltpetre until it was strong enough to float a raw egg. We very rarely bought meat. Col always killed his own meat. And we'd make our own bacon and hang it up to the ceiling of the kitchen on hooks. Because we had our own meat, sausages were a great novelty to us. The bus used to come out once a week and other people always got their fresh meat on Thursday night. And there'd be sausages for Thursday. Well, Heather, being cunning, would find an excuse to go to Auntie Syl's because she knew they were having sausages. I knew why she was going and she'd sneak home with a lovely big fat sausage in a piece of newspaper!

Another thing we always had for the winter was a big cask with about four or five hundred muttonbirds. They were salted, not skinned like we get now, and they were flat like a plate, cut open straight down the breast and opened out.

In the early days there was no such thing as gum boots and there was so much mud in the cow yard, where we had to get the cows in. There was logs, they were flattened a bit, to jump from one place to another. When we'd come from

The farm

the cowshed we'd just turn the tap in our kip boots. They were real heavy. We'd scrub them under the tap and put them upside down on the picket fence. We only had the one pair. If they dried they'd be hard and if they didn't dry they'd be wet. Col had these very, very heavy leather boots and he'd take them off of a night and dry them by the fire, and they'd be as hard as hard. But he used to keep them soft by rubbing them with oil or beeswax or mutton fat. He used to mix mutton fat with beeswax. He had big blocks of it and he used to warm it, light the candle and warm it against the flame, so that it was soft. It made them waterproof. But they'd get terribly hard, especially when they started to get a bit old.

We would gravel the yard afterwards, but the gravel would get buried sometimes, if there'd be lots of mud carted onto the top of the gravel. There was no concrete or anything. It was all red dirt. It didn't take many cow tracks to stir it up. There would perhaps be mud two feet deep, but there was generally a track round the fence that you could get to. You could scramble around hopping from clod to clod. The first rubber boots were wonderful things. Up until then we'd just have an old pair of shoes that we'd wear, and hardly ever any stockings.

But we didn't have the cows coming in early like they do now. The cows wouldn't be coming in until September anyway. Now they have them coming in all the year round. Most of the herds are coming in in June or July now, but we used to have ours coming in in late September or even October. And then there'd be the flush of the season with the heavy pastures. Mostly we turned ours out in about May and we nearly always had that three months spell through the winter.

We didn't get the vet very often. Every farmer was his own vet really. Col dealt with most things himself. He had more confidence in himself than in anybody else. He dosed his calves with phenyle for lung worm before he turned them out, and years later when I told that to some farmers they just wouldn't believe me. They reckoned that wasn't right at all. But it was right. Heather used to help Dad do it. Just before we turned them out onto the grass, while they were still on the bucket, he used to put a tablespoon of phenyle into their feed and they'd drink it. You'd only do it once, certainly, but they'd never get the lung worm that other calves did. Another thing he used was saltpetre and that was for a cow that got redwater. Well, if you said that now, people would think that you had poisoned it. But we always seemed to have our own remedies for everything.

After milking we'd always have to go back to the dairy and get the milk for the calves. They were in Gran's paddock over behind the house and we'd have to carry it right out through the big gate, the farm gate and across the road, to feed six or seven calves. Col was very, very tall and he had long arms and long legs and he used to cut the tops out of all these kerosene cans and put a plain fencing wire handle bent up into them. That was all right for him, but they were always dragging on the ground for us.

When we came down to the post office in 1930, we had an old cow we called Mottle. She had a disfigured udder and teats where she was burnt in the 1914 bushfire. She was a beautiful old cow. Eighteen's a long time for a cow. They hardly ever lived that long. They lived a hard life like the rest of us, I suppose.

Chapter 11

Building the dunny

"Sufficient unto the day."

Ruby

Pearl and I had a great friend, Mrs Hardy. We were older, but her and Pearl were more like sisters than anybody could be. Whatever we did, she was in it. If we papered a room, we'd do it together. She came and helped Pearl spring-clean Mother's. We'd do a day in Pearl's garden, a day in hers and a day in mine. And it was the three of us that built the dunny.

You'd go right down the yard with the dunny. You wouldn't have one near the house. It wasn't polite. People wouldn't just go in and out. If anybody was about they'd go round the other way or pretend they were getting a log from the wood heap. The wind had blown Pearl's dunny over. Cliff was that slow and while he was trying to get some boards to build a decent one, she was without and got desperate. So this day we decided we'd build the dunny and I went up early in the morning.

We had nothing to start with, but Pearl had a big wash house out from the house. So we decided we'd build it up against this as a lean-to. We wanted a long post to put the back on and found a piece of blackwood. It was a terrific length and I had to saw it and we only had an old saw. We had a basin of dripping and every now and again when the saw wouldn't go, we'd rub a bit of dripping on each side. It took me a terrible time, a good hour, this wood, it was so old and so seasoned and hardened dry. We wanted the post on a bit of a slope for the roof. Well, eventually we got it right and we dug holes and put the other posts in.

There was an old shed down the paddock. One side had blown in, so we carried these great long slabs home. We sawed them all up for the walls and made the place for a seat and left a doorway. I sawed the hole for the seat and it was square. But talk about hard wood. I think it was petrified! It was the hardest thing I ever did in my life – sawing that wood!

Mostly you put a trapdoor at the back to pull the pan out. Well, we didn't. We left it open at the front to take it out that way. Then we had to put a roof on it. I was the only one who knew how to put shingles on and I don't think I knew much. You put two together, then put another one over where they joined, overlapping. We wanted it done before Cliff got home and it was five o'clock when we finished. It took three of us a whole day and Mrs Hardy had to go home and have a bath. We found an old potato bag, opened it up and tacked that across for the door. Then we found an old chipped chamber with holes in it and we filled this with nasturtiums and put it on the roof. And that's the truth.

We used to get novelettes, 'penny dreadfuls'. There was one Grandma Porteus always bought and I still read them if I've got them. They were the cleanest, most wholesome reading and very funny. They all had stories and recipes. You'd pay a penny a week a copy. They were mostly printed on pink paper with a pink and blue cover. The pages were about six or nine inches long, just right for toilet paper. The kids weren't allowed to read them, but Madge used to sneak down there and you could piece them together if you stayed there long enough. Merle was a champion at that, always when the washing up had to be done.

There were snakes there too. Col hauled one out of the well in the bucket and I had to help him. When the kids wanted to go to the toilet, which was away down the paddock at the end of a big log, they were allowed to have one match to strike in case there were any spiders on the seat. But they always had to bring back the burnt-out match, so that I knew it was out.

But it was a long way down the paddock and always a big hole, a cesspit, no septic tank. They were all right if they were kept nice. You

Building the dunny

had to put lime or ashes down. When we moved to the post office there was only one with a can. So Col had a pit dug. The toilet was there before the hole was dug, and the trouble was a great big pine tree, the most beautiful tree, but they couldn't dig the hole straight down. So he put a slide down, a piece of tin a bit to one side. Two little kittens got down there one night and we had to get them out.

Madge was sitting there one day and happened to look down through the cracks in the floor. The boards were about an inch apart. She saw this great big snake and thought, 'What shall I do?' So she eased herself up onto the seat, stood up, opened the door and sprang. Anyway, they killed it. It was huge, and it looked so big, crawling about under the floor.

We had a new toilet built over at the bottom of the garden and one day young Col and another little fellow were playing down there. They were only about three. This little boy was terribly terribly shy and he came up and was standing at the door trying to get something out. Eventually he said there was a snake and Col was watching it. Col had said to him, 'I'll watch it and you go up and tell Mum'. But he was so shy, he had to get his courage up. A huge snake it was. By the time I got down there this snake was trying to climb the pear tree. I killed him with a garden hoe.

Another night there was a snake in the bedroom. It was just getting dark and Dad had just had a bath. We had a bath we used to scald all the pigs that got killed in Trowutta. It was that big. And we took a bath in the bedroom. He'd left his boots, his pants were hanging on the bed, and he'd gone off. I was milking the cows and Madge came over. She was trembling.

She saw this big snake go in the bedroom and she jumped out the window and came to me. So I went over and the cat was at the door, doubling its back, all hunched and its fur all up, looking in. I thought, 'Well, anyway', and I couldn't see anything, it was too dark. We had no electric light. So I had to get a candle and I got Father's slipper, put some wax in it and stood the candle up in it while I looked for the snake.

We had a big old cupboard about six feet long and four inches off the floor. And I could see the snake's head on one side and his tail the other, it was that long and thick. I got the axe. I could see him under there and his tail was about six inches out. I had to give him a touch with the candle so as he'd crawl out. And as he did I chopped his head off, got him right on the back. I got him all right. A tiger snake.

I killed two snakes in the house.

One night I was bathing the two little ones, Merle and Lilian, and I had sent Heather to get the soap. It was outside on a bench where we washed and Heather got out there and heard this thing hissing. So she came back and said, 'I can't find the soap'. And I said, 'It's out there, I know'.

I always encouraged my children not to be afraid of anything, so Heather went out again, and could still hear this thing hissing. She came back and said, 'I can't find it', telling this fib because she was frightened to go any further. Then minutes later, this snake came in the back door.

Ruby Paul outside her house and store with a black snake she killed

I'd gone out to get the soap and it crawled in ahead of me. Lilian was in the bath and I sung out to all of them to get up on the table. The snake wasn't nearly as big as the other one and it went in behind the door. And I chopped him up there.

Col always told me not to use an axe. It was dangerous because you were too close to the snake. It was too short in the handle and they'd spring. But I always did, because I thought I'd get one blow with the axe and it was the end. I wanted to chop the snake's head off if I could. If you hit them with a stick you don't always kill them.

The biggest snake I've ever seen was a tiger snake. It was on Sawleys' place and it was curled up. It was really as thick as your arm. I'd never seen such a big snake and I had Minnie, just a baby, out for a walk. I was on the road and Frank ran down a little track playing for quite a while. When I went to get him this big snake was curled up on the track between him and me. It was the biggest snake I've ever seen and I just had to let it crawl away. I couldn't bash it with the baby, could I?

Once I cracked a stick over Col's ankle, but he never knew what happened. We lived in a place where there were a lot of rats and they bored right through the wall. Of course the houses were not very well

Building the dunny

built, scrim and paper lined with boards, sometimes an inch between each board, and if a rat got in, he got in. I said, 'We'll have to do something about these rats, because they're trying to make a nest in my hair'.

There were three big holes in this tiny little room and this night I said, 'The rats are trying to pull my hair out'. So he got out of bed and plugged these three big holes. I'd made the wardrobe across the corner with a curtain on a stick. So I pulled the curtain down and used the stick to kill one rat. Colin killed another and next morning he said, 'My word, I've got a sore ankle. I reckon I knocked it on the bed'. I never let on I cracked the stick over his ankle killing this other rat.

The day Old Colonel, the bull, was in the garden he tried to get out and couldn't, so he jumped the fence. Even for old Colonel it was a good big jump over the gooseberry bushes and over the fence and he landed at the end of the drain. We had an open drain from the kitchen and every time they dug it, it got wider. So it was like a swamp where the drain finished.

That was where he landed, turned a half somersault, landed on his head, with his horns caught in the mud. And he couldn't get up. He was suspended. Myrtle and Harold, they'd come from the West Coast, and their kids had hardly even seen cattle, so with this bull stuck in the mud you can imagine the panic. Myrtle came running in. 'Oh Rube! Rube!' she was saying.

Then there was the day when two calves got their heads caught in the cream can. And we couldn't get them out. We pulled and we

Ruby of Trowutta

pushed and we just could not get them out. So we had to send for this old farmer who lived next door. He was a real old bush vet, a hard case. There was only one way to get them out. I had to push one calf in while he pulled the other one out. It was a narrow-necked cream can and they were both pulling. I had to push one in to make room for the other fellow to pull his head out. It was like a zigzag. Where one calf zigged, the other had to zag.

Much later, one Sunday morning, a little boy got stuck in a cream can. His mother had gone to church and his father was working in a paddock a mile away. It was a terrible hot day and these two kiddies were left playing, and the baby was asleep in a cot. Pearl, her son Cliff and I were in his car and a little girl ran out onto the road and said, 'Could you please help get my brother out of the cream can?'

They were playing hide and seek, and he jumped into the cream can, which was narrow-necked, of course. It was blazing hot and he was in a terrible state. We tried everything. Cliff looked in his car, got an axe and tried to get him out. When we found we couldn't, we knew we'd have to go for help. So we carried him into the shade and poured cold water over the can. They'd been playing in this black soil, he had no shoes on and his feet were black as ink. And he was crying. He was terrified. So were we. Cliff went for the boy's father and I rang the garage but nobody was there. So I rang Joyce Kay at the post office and she said, 'I'll see if I can get Mr Von Bibra to open the garage and you can cut him out with some of their cutters'.

So that's what they did. They put the cream can in the car and at the garage they cut the bottom out of it with an acetylene torch and just lifted it off him. His feet were that dirty and he looked that grubby. And I said, 'I hope you told them he wasn't yours'. And Cliff said, 'I made pretty sure of that'. He had an icecream and he was quite all right, though his face and hands were still as black as black. 'Sufficient unto the day is the evil thereof', Myrtle said.

Having the phone was a boon that day. When we first got it on, Auntie Syl was six. And we were seven. Dad's big cane chair always sat in the same position right beside the fireplace and the phone was on the wall just above.

Building the dunny

One Christmas we were all short of money – it was in the Depression – but Pearl got enough paper to do her kitchen for five shillings. And I got enough to do mine for seven and sixpence. But mine was a big room with eleven-foot walls and a hardwood dado about four feet high. The rooms had hardwood ceilings. And my word, it was hard work papering. Dad used to put a chair on top of the table, and if they were lucky they'd get two chairs up with a board between them. Mostly you could reach it off the table, especially if you were long in the arms. You could probably do it in an afternoon. That's so long as you had the room ready, all the furniture moved.

Pearl loved big rooms and she wanted to pull a wall out and make two rooms into one. Cliff said, 'You couldn't do it'. So she got a carpenter, Cec Haines, and he looked at it and said, 'You couldn't do it'. So she waited and got another carpenter, Tom Button. And he said he could do it with a five by five beam. So she rang up the mill and got the boss and told him she wanted a blackwood beam. And she said, 'You needn't say who it's for either'. So the boss said 'All right', and he went and told Cliff he wanted this five by five beam cut, and Cliff, as soon as he heard what he had to do, he knew. And they brought this beam and dropped it off at the gate and he had to carry it in! Anyway, she made a most beautiful room of it. A beautiful dining room. It was the best built house in Trowutta in those days.

Heather helped me milk twelve cows. The pig yard was miles away from the dairy and I had to cart the buttermilk in kerosene cans. It was always thick and curded after standing in the sun, horrible and smelly, and the buckets all got coated. There was a picket fence and it had gradually sunk into the mud. Dad could always step over it because he was a very big man. But I had to climb up on a box that I'd put on the outside. And the pig'd come along on the inside, an old sow. And I would tread on her back, she was so quiet, and give her a scratch. One day some dogs came from nowhere and started to fight and the pig shot from underneath and left me on my back in this mud, this smelly slurry, with the buckets of buttermilk all over the top of me! I couldn't get up for laughing.

One time I got a burning coal down my boot. They were short gumboots, with two tabs at the back with eyelets and they tied. And I tied them in a knot instead of a bow. I was carrying this shovel of hot coals and I tripped. The coals went down the back of my boot and I couldn't get it untied! And there was me, squealing and laughing at the same time! And Heather had to run and get the butcher's knife to cut the string at the back!

Just after Pearl's husband died she wasn't sleeping and I went over to sleep with her. We only lived across the road. She was on one side of the room and I was on the other. And when she was going to bed she put this sleeping tablet on the dressing table between us. When she took off her blouse the button came off and she put it on the table too. Well, that night she couldn't sleep, so she just grabbed the tablet, as she thought, and swallowed it down with a drink of water. Then she went to sleep and slept for six hours. And when she got up the tablet was still there, but the button was gone!

And that's the real truth. Everything I've told you is the truth.

6-pint cooking pot

Chapter 12

Housekeeping and homemaking

"You did whatever you had to do. A day was never long enough to do all I wanted."

Ruby

The house at Nesdale had two rooms and a skillion. The skillion was the kitchen and the back bedroom. And we added a back porch. That was something special, made out of split palings, done when Dad wasn't there. When he came home he didn't know how to get in. The door had disappeared!

First of all when we were married we bought an iron bedstead, and a table and six chairs. We had one cane chair, a sort of an easy chair. It would've done me for nearly a lifetime, but Colin was too heavy for it. They weren't well made because they soon fell to pieces.

The first curtains I had when I got married were lace, very long, two pair, one for the bedroom and one for the sitting room, big and heavy, and they had waratahs in the pattern. And Mrs Frost, she was nearly one of the family before ever Pearl and Cliff were married, she bought me a beautiful white counterpane for a wedding present, a marcella quilt.

We had a chiffonier of dark varnished wood with a fancy back, and that was where I kept all the good china. And I built wardrobes out of timber and put curtains round them. One was a bit crooked but it hung our clothes all right. Then there was a big cupboard made of tongue and groove scrap timber. It was our linen press. All the kiddies' clothes and things were put in little heaps. Each had their own space and all the house linen went into it. It seemed to hold everything.

I had a beautiful old dresser made of heavy white pine with a rack for the plates, wide at the bottom for big plates, then saucers and small plates, and hooks for cups all along each row. But it was so hard to keep clean, I varnished it. We had a beautiful high chair made out of figured hardwood, such a pretty light colour. We had a blackwood one for Madge, and bought this other one for Heather at a sale. It did Lilian, Merle and Col. We loaned it to several other families, then Heather used it for her girls and her grandchildren. Now one of her daughters uses it for her grandson. And Madge still has the other one.

We had Frank Sawley's cot for years, for all the five children. Harry Butler made it. It was beautiful. They didn't get sawn timber from the mills then. They just cut the timber out and adzed it square. It was all hand dressed. It had square corner posts and wooden side frames. They had a series of holes drilled into them and they were threaded with plain fencing wire in three rows overlapping, like iron garden guards. It was really a nice looking cot. The base was interlaced iron slats. In those days the hay bales had iron strapping, flat wire-like slats, which they used. Then you'd put a tick on that.

We used to get beautiful pine boxes which held two tins of kerosene. I had three or four put together with dovetail joints, and nailed them to the wall and put a cretonne curtain in front. We had them for dressing tables too. You'd cut a square of material and fit it at the top, then you'd make this nice big wide frill. Mother always had white hailstone muslin. Then you'd put a cloth over that with crochet about three inches wide all round. Then you just sat the mirror on it.

We used butter boxes too. We called them 'out-of-the-way boxes' for our kiddies. I padded lids for them, put a cretonne frill round and they used to throw all their toys in them. Much later, for Madge's and Heather's girls, I got petrol drums, cleaned them out, covered them and made them into little stools.

We had a beautiful figured blackwood double bed, handmade out of local timber, with panels at head and foot, which was Heather's. It was very high and it used to creak, but it was a beautiful piece of timber. The big dining room table we had at the post office was about three feet wide and about six feet long and it was only one board. It was a good big table and it's standing in the Smithton kindergarten now.

At Nesdale there used to be a pine table out in the porch and every Saturday we had to scrub the pine. Of course a lot of the furniture was pine. We had to scrub it with sandsoap. We did a lot of work on that table. We mostly had a big pastry board, it would be nearly half the size of the table. It had a frame round the back and it sloped so that you could roll along the edges and the flour didn't push off. You'd always do your pastry work on that.

And the chairs. All the chair legs had to be scrubbed on Saturday. Maggie Burke still talks about that. She says she never saw anybody put the kitchen chairs all out in the yard. We always did that. We used ashes in the very early days to scrub our kitchen table, but we got sandsoap soon after. I used to make most of our own soap because we killed our own meat and there was a lot of fat. We only used it for the men's trousers and scrubbing the floors.

You were always scrubbing to keep the floors clean. They were wooden and they used to get very dirty. You'd just get down and scrub the boards and they'd look lovely when they were done. If you had two or three boards at the back door that was all. We had a step cut out of a log. There was no concrete in the early days. We had boards that we used to walk out into the yard, to track out. If we wanted a mat it was usually a washed potato bag. They'd wash up beautifully white, creamy coloured. You'd have one in front of the fire and one by the door usually, and the rest would be boards, or lino later on. They used some sort of dyes to brand the potato bags with and we'd paint over them and make a pattern on it. There was a stuff called congoleum that came in. It was very cheap and it was beautiful, you hardly had to polish it. But if you dragged the leg of a chair or a table along it you'd tear it. You got squares for the bedroom. It was quite good so long as you didn't drag the bed across it. But the pattern used to wear off.

We used bar soaps, Bluebell or Nutbrown for washing the clothes. When the kids were little I used to give them a bar and a hammer and some nails and they used to hammer the nails into the soap. We had those tin tubs with handles on either end. We had a big one which the adults bathed in, but you also did your washing in it. And there was a smaller one used mainly for the children and we could stand in that and have a stand-up wash because you didn't have the water to spare.

Once I had Madge all dressed for church in a white velvet bonnet and white embroidery dress and she had white shoes and socks. Minnie Sawley was there, she was three, about thirteen months older than Madge, and I had them both ready for church. I was in the bedroom and I heard them giggling and Minnie had kidded Madge to get in the bath, socks and all. I'd left the bath there and it was a temptation! When Mr May, the minister, came along – he used to drive us out in the gig – he had to wait while I found something to put on her – and it was nothing as glamorous as that!

I killed a rooster once and I didn't know how I was going to do it. Syl was sick, and I wanted to make something for her. So I put him under the bath with his head poking out to chop it off. And I missed his head and hit the bath. Once poor old Grandma was sick and Mother wanted a chook and I said, 'I'll get you one'. Col had only just bought these five big black purebred chooks. So I waited until he was in bed and went out to the fowl house. So it wouldn't squawk I held it by the beak and by the time I got to Mother's, I'd choked it and it was dead. So she just chopped the head off.

When we went to Roger River we bought a stove. It was a beautiful big stove. And all the women used to come in. I didn't think Colin minded, but every time he came home the house was always full of somebody cooking in my stove. And he said, 'I don't think that stove was a good idea'. Community stove. Everybody's Christmas cakes.

At Trowutta we had a Peters oven, it was a beautiful oven. You had to light the fire underneath it as well as on top. That oven was all set in stone and clay. The kids had to go away down the road and across another farm to get the pipeclay to clean the fireplace with. They'd dig it out with an old shovel and mix it up with water, then carry it home in the billy. And the hobs and all round were always white as anything.

If you didn't keep it done, all the clay would dry and come out. So you'd put a fresh dose on nearly every day. There was a log of wood about two feet long, just the width of the opening where you had the fire. That was always whitened, the same as the fireplace, and laid in front of the opening when you weren't using it. One day when I lit the fire under the oven there was a terrible commotion and the cat shot out. It was a lovely warm place for it to sleep when the fire was only lit on top. The log must have been pulled out and so the cat got in.

We had cranes then to use for cooking all the time and a big black frying pan with the handle over the top. All the saucepans used to hang up. That was one thing I had. I usually had pieces of chain and hooks made by blacksmiths in the smithy to hang the saucepans on. A lot of the utensils and things we had were better made than they are now, and different. They were iron saucepans and they mostly had hanging handles, because of your open fireplaces. When people got stoves they got saucepans with handles straight out.

And there was big fountains. We never had those, we had big black kettles. But when we came down to the post office there was a fountain. We used it for a while, but it had a crack in it. I was always calling Merle to fill the kettle and she said, 'It's a wonder you don't come up to school and sing out 'Merle, will you come and fill the kettle?'

We had flatirons that used to stand in front of the fire to get hot and of course they'd get all black. And there'd be miles of ironing with the starched tablecloths and all our starched petticoats and pinnies. And you used to have a piece of beeswax in a linen cloth and you'd rub the iron with that first and then with another polishing cloth and that would clear your iron. Every iron you picked up you rubbed with beeswax and then with a clean cloth, otherwise you'd get black on your linen. I can remember the smell of it now. It was a beautiful clean smell.

There were Coolgardie safes about, but they were fiddly things. We kept the meat tied up in a big pine tree. It was always in the shade and there's always a breeze in a pine tree. It would keep a fortnight, well that wasn't long to keep a sheep. People that killed a beast had to corn most of it. You'd buy a bit of fresh in between, but you'd practically live on corned beef all the winter. It got hot enough in the summer but we wouldn't worry about it. When we made our own butter it would keep whatever the weather. You'd always have a back porch with a safe in it. If the butter was going off we'd just make some more, because we always had cows. I had a dairy all my life.

I used to try and make one garment every night after tea. Having four little girls, it might be a little pair of pants, or just an apron or pinafore, or a baby bib. But one garment every night after tea I used to try and do. Or a shirt. None of them wore singlets. They had shirts and petticoats and occasionally a slip bodice to wear underneath because we didn't have cardigans. Many a time when I had to make their blouses and everything they wore at school I'd be sewing at two o'clock in the morning, especially if I had something special.

The kerosene lamp was on the table behind me. There was only the one and Dad'd be reading the paper by that too. And always this candle. As I shifted the material, I shifted the candle and moved it from one place to another as I'd do a seam on the old treadle machine. Well, Mother used to lend me hers. It was really supposed to be mine, but I never claimed it. They used to just bring this machine from her to me. Then when Lilian was coming that's when I got the 'Kangaroo'. It came from Chandlers in Melbourne out of a catalogue. The Singer parts fitted and it was called a Kangaroo because it was made here in Australia under licence. Singer was American. Madge has still got it and it still goes. It's just so big and the parts are worn so it's got to be nursed along a bit.

But the children learned to sew on it, they learned to treadle and they learned to make cords. Dad used to make his wallaby snares on it out of string. He'd wind them up into a cord and they'd treadle and he'd hold them. They were made on the wheel that you wound the bobbin with. The spools weren't the little round ones, they were long and fitted into a shuttle. You'd hook the twine with a hairpin or piece of wire onto one of the machine spokes and Dad or somebody at a distance held the other end of the folded string and gradually moved back while one of the kids treadled. They did that in all the old homes here towards the winter, when you'd be snaring for wallabies and possums.

I made gowns for babies. Little white muslin gowns. I always made Mrs Hardy's babies' gowns, and Mrs Burke's and Mrs Rundle's. And I used to cut out gowns for other people, even at Scotchtown before I was married. I don't know how many layettes I made. I only had three gowns and I still used them for Merle because I didn't get her gowns finished. I had them cut out, but they were only partly made when I went to the hospital. Then I gave one to a woman who had nothing to bury her dead baby in. I made somebody a white petticoat for a school concert out of one, and Heather's white slippers for the concert out of the other. I'd nothing else. And the girls didn't have white shoes.

You had to do things and whatever you had to do, you'd think, 'Now what can I do that with?' And it'd just come to you. You'd look around and see what you had and what you could do with it, whether it was a bit of bag or a bit of string, whatever you had. You just did it. I made things like jiffies. I cut the pattern out of a piece of old paper and fitted that on Heather's foot. I had to make it up. And I put a bow on them. The only pattern I bought was when Madge was going away to school. I got a Madam Weigall's pattern for her blouses. I made a coat. I made a tunic. I made everything. I even made them hats.

I made a lot of bonnets. When motor cars first came out they used to call them 'motor bonnets' and they were very pretty. One bonnet I used to make had a straight piece to go along the face and you'd fold it and stiffen it with buckram. The crown would be gathered or pleated, and you'd pleat the stuff over the buckram to make it a bit fancy, and gather it a bit at the back, then you'd put a big bow or rosette and you tied it under the chin. And the inside was lined. They were well made. I made one for Heather once for a fancy dress parade. She got second prize in it. It was black velvet lined with pink silk tied with a big bow under her chin. And she hated it. It had pink rosettes on each side and everybody loved it on her because it showed off all her dark curls.

Merle was a rooster once in a concert. Col had bought some nice black Minorca chooks. He always had chooks for us, he was very proud of them. And I went out and chased a rooster and pulled its whole tail out. I made a beak with a bit of red stuff and put a comb on it of red material. It was a black suit, a black rooster. There was a hole for her head and it came down with two holes for her arms, and when she lifted them they looked like wings. And she'd crow. She wore a big pair of black bloomers. And it was a black rooster's tail. I don't know whether her father ever knew.

For Grandma and Grandfather Porteus's diamond wedding, I sent away for material and made them all little jumper suits of this lovely silk. Madge's was lemon and Heather's was a deeper gold. Lilian had burnt orange. Merle had a pretty little frock. I always made my own frocks too, not that I had many.

There was a children's ball. Heather had a white dress, a very ordinary white voile dress. And Auntie Phyllis sent some bunches of artificial grapes and cherries. So she had bunches of cherries hanging on each ear and beautiful big purple grapes right round the hem. We cut the fruit out of the labels of IXL jam and preserved fruit tins and pasted them all over the skirt and in big letters across the front, red bias binding on this white, we had 'EAT MORE FRUIT'. And she had a big headband, 'EAT MORE FRUIT'.

Madge was a lemon. She had a skirt of green crepe paper with half a big lemon on the front and a yellow crepe paper bodice, and her hat was half a lemon of yellow crepe paper with a great green leaf up each side. Lilian was Bo Peep and Merle was a fairy. The kids were always excited seeing things come together. But we never had cameras in those days, so we never took any photos. I made every stitch the girls wore right up until they went to high school, overcoats and all. We never had bought things.

A day was never long enough to do all I wanted. When I only had one or two children and a couple of cows I had plenty of time. I did everything. You did whatever you had to do, you just didn't take any notice. Whatever came up to do, you did it, and if you were tired you didn't take any notice, you just shrugged your shoulders and went on.

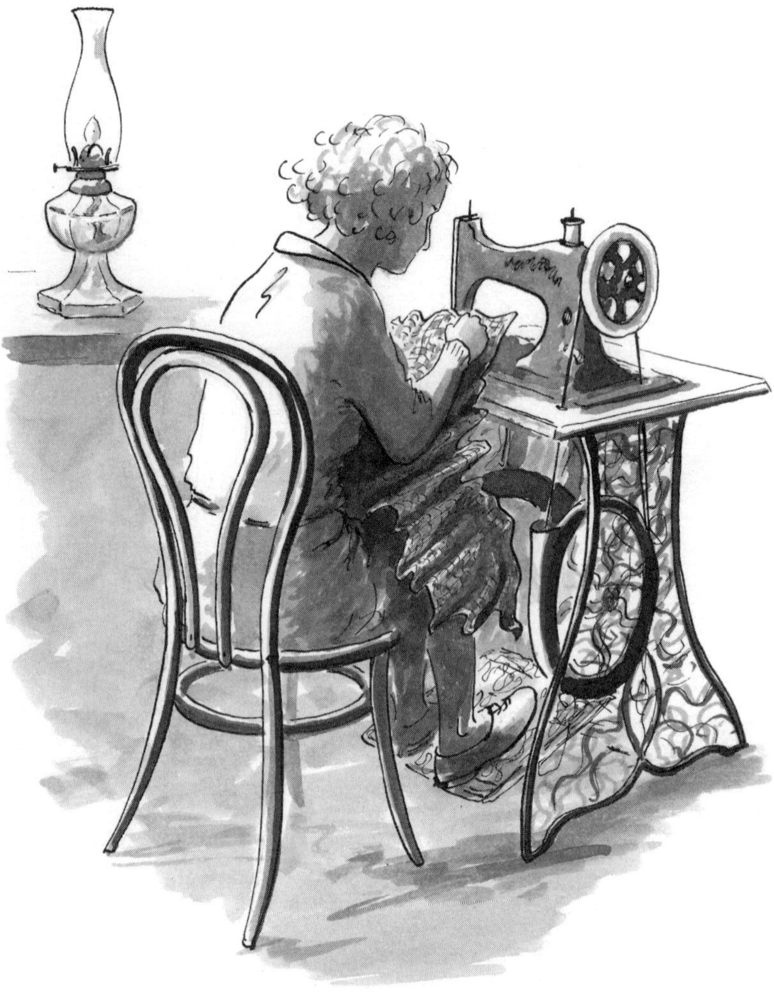

Chapter 13

Balls and bazaars

"We'd have a ball, because that's what we could do."

Ruby

The school at Trowutta was opened in 1915. Mr Kel Snare was the first headmaster but he wasn't there for more than six months. He joined up for the war. The next was Mr Mason. He only stayed a matter of weeks before he joined up too. Then we never had another male teacher for years. They sent girls from then on, and it was a long way back to send girls. One came and we didn't know who she was. She never got a letter all the time she was in Trowutta and we thought she was a spy.

Mrs Crole boarded the teacher. Somebody had to do it. You had to provide for the teachers, but they paid their board. It was good pay. Various ones boarded the teachers. It's not always a good idea to have a teacher where you've got schoolchildren either. I never did it while our children were at school.

One of these teachers arrived in Irishtown at half past ten at night on the train. She'd been told she could go right to Edith Creek by train, but they didn't tell her she had to stop the night in Irishtown. And there she landed and there was no place for her. There was only a boarding house where a lot of working men boarded.

It was one of those pouring nights with heavy hail showers. And she was standing there on the station with her tin trunk and she didn't know what to do or where to go. Then this man carrying a box on his shoulder, put it down for a spell when she asked him, and he said, 'I'll take you home to the Missus'. So he took her home to the missus. And next day they took her out to the school. And she boarded with my auntie and uncle at Edith Creek.

There was one small school room at Trowutta and seven classes in the one room. There was one teacher and over the years numbers ranged from fifteen students to probably twenty-six or twenty-seven. Sometimes if the weather was nice some classes would sit outside, with the responsible students in charge. The teacher still had to keep her eye on them. It must have been very difficult.

When the children got the measles they each had to stay away from school for three weeks after the spots went, which meant over a month for each one. And while it was in the house nobody from that house was allowed to go to school. I had Phyl's two kids and Syl's Minnie as well as Heather and Lilian, so by the time Madge got back to school she was nearly eight. The first day they went back to school, Heather came home saying, 'My sister was top'. Because we'd always read with them and try to teach them and do little adding-ups and things.

Madge went away to secondary school in Devonport when she was just twelve, and when she was eleven and Heather was nine we planted trees in the school ground. It was a cold rainy day with these sleety showers coming from the south-west. Dear, it was cold. You'd see these big black clouds coming and it'd start to rain, these haily showers, and they'd make a run for it, straight into school, then Heather'd go back out again because she was determined to get those trees in. She got them planted and just about every one grew, so she must have made a fairly good job of digging the holes. They were only tiny, some would not have been any more than twelve inches high. They grew to giant pines. Now they're flat. Cut down.

Heather was nearly fourteen when she left school and carried her chair home. In her last year they were short of desks, and being one of the bigger students she sat up at the teacher's table and had her books on a corner. She'd carried her chair up on her back to school. So the day she left she carried it home.

Not long after she left, a man teacher came and Heather went up and asked him for the job teaching sewing, because she knew he wouldn't be able to do that. So she was teaching kids to sew soon after she left school for a whole afternoon a week and got four shillings and threepence for that.

We had one crochet needle in our house and I used to crochet round the edge of things I made. Heather was always fascinated by the needle going in and out and when I put it down she'd sneak it while I was doing something else. I didn't knit that much, so we never had skeins or balls of wool. But we always had a big plait of darning wool and that hung on the mantelpiece, with the darning needle in it. Heather used to sneak a thread from it and the crochet needle and hide under the big bed, and that was where she learned to crochet. She used to knit Dad's socks for him. He had bad legs with varicose veins and he was a tall man with big long shins and he could never get socks long enough. So she used to knit socks for him and put five skeins into a pair of socks.

For the school concerts each child would have about seven different costumes. The teacher and I used to sew costumes every night and we'd finish up the evening with a cup of tea and bread and prune jam, warming our feet in the oven. One year they did *Caller Herrin'* and we made creels out of big Weetie boxes. We covered them with white paper and drew the latticework on them. That year we used kippered herrings but they smelled too much. So next year we cut out cardboard fish and painted them with silvafros.

One year when Heather was quite small there was a school concert item where the kids had one big bundle of sticks. One kid tried to break it but couldn't, then two tried together but couldn't, and so it went on. At last every child took several sticks from the bundle and all broke them at once, chanting 'Unity is strength'.

We had a big bazaar once a year, sometimes for the church, sometimes for the school, but mostly for the hall. In the early days we always had one for the church, what you would call a fair nowadays. We'd hold a meeting to start with and go round everybody and say, 'Now what are you going to give me for my stall?' And we'd make something for each other. Everybody gave something to the others' stalls.

I used to have a sweet stall and I nearly always took down my bedroom curtains and put them up at the stall. We used a lot of crepe paper, we'd get a fair bit cheap to cover the stalls. Coloured paper, streamers, fringes and all sorts, every stall was decorated and it'd be beautiful to walk into the hall. We'd work for it for weeks and weeks and weeks. All these home-made lollies.

I made coconut ice and toffees and fudge and snowballs and marshmallows and stuffed dates. And if we could get walnuts, two halves of a walnut with some filling. Turkish delight was beautiful. Barley sugar we used to make. Before we started to cook, a day before if the kids were home, we'd make this big batch of barley sugar so that the kids could have a go at that. It was cheap and we put it in patty papers and shapes. We used to do butterscotch and caramel and for nights we'd make baskets for the sweets. We'd save up our tea packets and the kids would cut them in half and cover them with crepe paper.

There was a fancy stall, produce, cakes and everything. Pearl always had the fancy stall. We used to make bag aprons and oven cloths and bag towels. We bought sugar in seventy-pound bags and there was never one of those bags wasted. There were always bag towels in our homes and in the dairies. They'd wash up. Once they'd been washed a couple of times and all that hair and fibre was washed out, they were really quite good. After they'd been boiled a couple of times they'd be quite soft. There was always one bag hanging where you'd wash when you came in from the garden, because Trowutta was red dirt, very red.

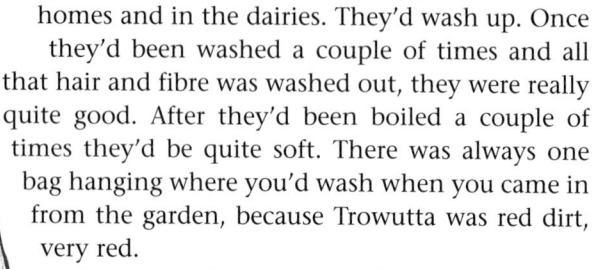

I sent two bag aprons I'd made to Minnie Sawley in Melbourne. One had a Dutch mill and the other a big basket of tulips cut out and appliqued. We used bag aprons in the garden and scrubbing floors and everything. Sometimes you'd just trim them up with bands, edging strips of nice-coloured material. We used a lot of bias binding on the oven cloths and towels. Peg bags and pot holders too, trimmed with cretonne, even embroidery and sometimes drawn threadwork.

At the harvest festivals we'd generally have a concert and a sale. In the early days Col was always the auctioneer. Later I used to do a lot of auctioneering. I was a real good auctioneer. I used to do it at the CWA and all those things. There'd be vegetables at the harvest festival, but people used to bring all sorts of other things, anything they thought would sell, cases of good tinned fruit. There'd always be a lot of bread. And they'd run each other up.

And we had a hat trimming competition for the men. Dave McDonald won it once. His wife Cissy had a hat with a big pink rose. And I said to Dave, 'Just stick that rose straight up the back of your hat'. So she pulled the hat off her head and took this great big rose and stuck it up the back of his hat with a fancy pin she had. And Dave got the prize because they thought he was very clever.

Whenever I get the smell of kerosene I think of those country dances at Trowutta. Old Bill Walters – he had a wooden leg – he used to prepare the floor, light the lamps and lock up afterwards. They were Tilley lamps until the power came through. He used to cut up candles into sawdust and put it in the oven and when the candle was all through the sawdust, then he'd mix it with kerosene and do up the floor so that it was slippery. You'd come to the hall door and you could smell that kerosene.

We always took all the kids. From the time Merle could walk she loved to dance. She did the charleston with Madge when she was very little. I always took them to every dance I could. I always said, 'Well, I wasn't let go when I was young'. And I was the only one who couldn't dance. I never did learn. I suppose I would've if Colin had been a dancer. But he wasn't. He could do all the sets, but he didn't like dancing. And as he got a bit older he used to get a nose bleed every time he danced. If he turned around twice his nose would start to bleed.

He was the auctioneer for years and years at our sale of gifts and harvest festivals. But he got to the stage where about halfway through he'd always have a nose bleed. After the auction they'd clear everything away and have a dance. Nothing was ever done except that you had a dance afterwards. And everybody went to those dances, everybody. There was always a row of kids asleep on the anteroom floor or up on the stage. They'd have rugs and pillows and the parents would dance. No wonder the children learnt to dance, because as they got a bit older they graduated from the anteroom floor to the hall. They'd run a ball for the children till 10 o'clock, then give them their supper out in the anteroom, and then the adults 'd take over for the rest of the night.

Usually the balls were in aid of something – sometimes for the school, sometimes for the hall, or one of the churches or sports, the cricket probably. When there'd be an appeal out for funds, we'd have a ball, because that was what we could do.

The first adult fancy dress ball Pearl dressed as Night. And Uncle Cliff, he was the village idiot. He wore an old shirt and chewed a carrot. There was a lady who made her dress out of a chaff bag. She cut it in a sort of loose Magyar style and trimmed it with pink satin applique round the neck. I always think she used her wedding frock, because when she was married she wore a very pretty pink satin frock. Perhaps it might have been a piece left over from it. Anyway she got a prize that night, for the costume that cost the least. It was just like a frock, but who would have thought of it! She and her husband were beautiful dancers. He was the most glorious dancer. There was no jigging or anything. He danced every step of every dance, and some of those dances they used to do, the old-time dances, were very complicated.

We had anybody we could get for the music, ranging from the fiddle and piano and accordion. Anybody who could play, usually just by ear. We had no records. Sometimes we used to pay a pianist to come from Smithton, or sometimes we'd even get a two- or three- piece orchestra. But mostly, just for ordinary dances we'd have an accordion. When the Finnegans came round from Gormanston, Molly Finnegan she played for nothing for years and years. She could play too.

Then there was another lady used to come out from Irishtown to play for us, a Mrs Alice Scott. She used to play by ear. Her daughter lived in Stanley and she played all the latest tunes. She'd hear this piece at her daughter's and she'd say, 'Don't speak to me', and she'd go straight down and get on the train and travel home from Stanley to Irishtown. She lived just behind the station and she said she was terrified somebody would come and speak to her. But she went straight home and sat down at the piano and played the piece through and then she said it didn't matter. But if anybody had spoken to her that would have been the end of it. She had to start right over again from scratch.

The anteroom was a little back room that the ladies used as a powder room. It was half the width of the back of the hall. The other half was the kitchen and there was a partition in between. We made our coffee in kerosene tins over an open fire. Auntie Pearl always made the coffee. There was two tins went on, one was tea and one was coffee. The cups belonged to the hall. They were in big pine boxes. The seats would be all round the hall and the men would take the box of cups round first, then another man would take the kerosene tin of tea and another would follow with the coffee. They'd go round dipping it out with a billy as they went, out of these black kerosene tins. Somebody would follow up with the sugar and the milk, they'd take it in turn. Then the ladies would come round with the sandwiches.

Sometimes the kids used to offer to take the sugar round. The cups that had had the handles knocked off them were our sugar basins, with one spoon in it. You'd go round and if you wanted sugar you got to stir as you went. And this was at a ball and you'd be all dressed up in your finery, but you still helped to serve the supper and wash up after it. Everybody put their shoulder to the wheel. It was a wonderful feeling of fellowship. And everybody took the supper.

Balls and bazaars

It was nearly always 'Ladies a basket and men a shilling'. There was a girl who was noted for her basket. She used to roll her shoes in a teatowel and change them when she got to the hall, and that was her basket! One night she'd brought a bottle of milk and one of the fellows tipped the milk out and filled the bottle with water, so that day she brought a bottle of water. She used to get a bit of red crepe paper and soak it in water to do her cheeks up, and girls used to use cornflour for powder.

And then there'd be the little gossips, and 'You wouldn't think this one would do that'. I remember a man coming up to me and he said, 'You know, Mrs Paul, Shirley's dress doesn't leave much to the imagination, does it?' It was pretty tight. There was another family of four sisters – their mother used to make their clothes too and they were always up with the latest. One was a fairly big girl and when strapped evening frocks came in, Heather was dancing with one boy who said, 'Gee, I wish her braces would break'.

At Roger River the old mill hall had once been a barn or a storage shed. It had a beautiful myrtle floor. That part of it was lovely. We all used to go to the dances there. Professor Mackay used to go himself. But being an old barn there were no facilities at all. They'd provided for the ladies with an old chamber pot. Its handle had been knocked off and there was a big chip on one side of it. But there were still some beautiful pink flowers on the outside. And we all used it. Took it outside and emptied it. Madge never used it. The girls would go in there into the little back room two at a time, because one had to keep nit at the door while the other one used it.

When the electricity came through to Trowutta in 1951 we had a 'Switch-On Ball', an opening ball. They had a big notice up with these big yellow stripes, like something was switched on. That was a great night. Everybody had ball dresses. Heather had a beautiful red dress, heavy red satin. That was the biggest ball I think I've ever seen.

A circus set up in the station yards at Roger River once. They'd get as close to the station as they could, because that's how they'd travel, by the train. Dad nearly always took the kids to the circus. It was in Irishtown one time, and another time in the station yards at Smithton. But any of those travelling shows must have been very difficult. One came to Trowutta and they had booked the hall. In the afternoon somebody went round to check and said how uncomfortable it must be for them because one woman was cutting up steak on the end of the table and at the same table someone was putting on make-up, getting ready for the night. Wouldn't that be awful? Steak and make-up all mixed up!

At one time somebody used to bring pictures out to Trowutta and show them. They had the hall set up, but we didn't have them very often. It was a great occasion when we did. The old silent pictures with Charlie Chaplin and they stewed the boots and ate them. Silent pictures, they'd write the verse on and then you had to try and read the words, and I could never keep up with them. I very seldom went. I would stay home with the baby or the little ones. Later, when we had a car, Dad would always take the kids..

They had holes up in the end wall for the projection box. There was no ladder up to the little loft, but there was a cupboard, it might have been for the kerosene lamps. So they had to climb on top of the cupboard and lift themselves up through a hole in the ceiling to show the pictures while we were all sitting down in the hall in those hard seats.

Two different people used to bring the pictures to Trowutta at one time, O'Brien's and Campbell's, and we had an old gramophone for the sound effects. Croles had one that had the old cylinder records to wind up. Then Minnie Sawley had one. She can still sing bits out of the old records, *The Prisoner's Song* and *The Prisoner's Sweetheart*, and *Felix Kept on Walking*.

The first coloured picture I saw was *The Trail of the Lonesome Pine* and the colour in that was beautiful, the trees and all. That was in Trowutta. I remember when the first 'talkies' came. The first 'talkie' I saw was in Smithton, *The Street of Singers' Serenade*.

Quite a bit later, when the children got older we used to go to Smithton for the pictures occasionally, or to Stanley. All the good pictures came to Smithton. A big load of us went to see *Mrs Miniver* in the old hall at Smithton. And over the whole hall you could hear this sobbing sound. We were all crying. That was much later at the end of the Second World War. It really brought the war home to us.

The Trowutta Show started in 1934. They used to have log chops in the first shows, because that's when Mr Moore had a heart attack and died. I don't think he'd even got through the log. The blocks were all round the north side of the old hall. That's where they had the chopping, and the show was inside. After they moved the show down to the Recreation Ground, that's when they started having different things. They had all the pens for the stock built right down in the corner.

In latter years they had horse riding, dressage, feature races and a sort of a challenge match. Most of it is impromptu. Everyone would stand round and cheer. It was good fun. Heather won the ladies' man fern chop one year. She'll always have a go at anything.

Balls and bazaars

It was a show and a half, I can tell you. Cakes and jams and dairy products and eggs and homemade bread. And the flowers! The flowers were a treat. And sewing and knitting and all that sort of thing. It was a really good show in those days and everybody gave their all. People would have perhaps twenty or thirty entries, and they'd be up half the night and next morning preparing.

I'd be up before the sun rose, decorating baskets and things to put in the show. Decorated baskets! I got some of that pink myrtle from up Beattie's Hill and put it with autumn polyanthus. The judges said, 'That was a beautiful basket, but you shouldn't mix flowers with the bush'.

Mrs Walters made a pie for one of the early Trowutta shows. And when they were putting them out, poor old Charley Aitken dropped it. So he turned it up the other way and put the crust on it and she got the first prize! I remember Syl getting first prize for a pie once. I'd made an apple pie with a nice flaky crust about this high and she'd just made short crust and put a few leaves and things on it. I thought it was the flattest looking pie you ever saw, but that's just one person's opinion.

She put in a plateful of butterfly cakes once and she still talked about it, she told me again about it a few weeks before she died. You were supposed to put four or six of everything on a little plate. Grace only put six and Grace got the prize. So Syl went to the judge and said, 'I made a great big plateful and they looked lovely'. Grace's were nice and spongy and Syl's had great big holes in them. But Syl thought that because she had a big plateful she ought to get the prize.

In the early days some of those judges left a lot to be desired. Heather was always annoyed because I had been putting scones in the show and taking prizes for years and then along came a new judge, and my scones were put out because I'd cut them with a knife and not with a cutter. Really! I always cut my scones square in those days.

Heather was annoyed about the time when my Madeira cake was put out. The Madeira cake that I made, and always had made all my life, when it was raw, when it was just ready to go into the oven, I used to sprinkle icing sugar over it. That made this lovely sweet crunchy crust and that was a Madeira cake. And you could put strips of lemon peel across it. This was what the old recipe books used to say. But then my cake was put out because it had lemon peel on top. That was a real Madeira cake and I've still got the recipe. It was in the first Central Cookery Book. That was used in high school domestic science.

We used to get the lemon peel in big pieces, and we'd cut out a big circle and put two or three of these across the cake and sprinkle it with icing sugar. It used to rise and this crusty top used to have a little break across it in the centre. It always had to have this little break across it, and that was a real Madeira cake. But that's what it was put out for in the finish. I think Mrs Button put it out. She gave a fruit cake first prize. She cut the fruit cake and there was a big raw patch in the middle, yet she gave it first prize. She said it was a beautiful texture, the rest of it!

One year I made a crinoline cake. I made it in a big round basin – it was our dripping basin to tell you the truth, that I cooked it in. And we got a doll and cut it in half and stood it on the cake. We dressed the doll and iced the cake with white icing and trimmed it all up. Heather iced it and it was beautiful, really beautiful. And somebody told the judge, 'Oh,' she said, 'They only iced a block of wood there'.

So it was put out. And I tell you who was terrible offended about that – Uncle Will. He took our entries up. And he was right. If you saw the cake they gave first prize to! It was most ordinary and it was decorated with the brightest pink that school kids would do, just a little row round it. And this crinoline cake was gorgeous, beautifully done and trimmed up.

I nearly always got first for sausage rolls. And apple pies. But we never cared whether we took a prize or not. So long as the other stuff was good and we had a good show. That was the main thing. Different years you'd put different things in. Yeast buns and bread. Biscuits, chocolate cake, sponge cakes, Swiss roll, decorated cakes, Madeira cake and butterflies – nearly any of those things you'd take your share of prizes. There were some very good cooks and other people took their share of prizes too, but we used to enter a lot of things.

Rich fruit cakes and light fruit cakes, just with sultanas. You'd hardly know which to pick among such beautiful entries. Plum puddings, flowers and needlework. Heather always got a lot of these prizes. She used to get prizes in everything. She used to do a lot of needlework, and then in later times when she had a beautiful garden of her own, we took a lot of prizes with carnations and pansies and gladdies. And a lot of our vegetables used to take prizes. But it would depend a lot on what the weather was like just beforehand.

The show was at the end of February or the beginning of March, usually a long weekend at the beginning of March, or the last weekend in February. When we got the schedule we'd go right through it and everybody was so keen they'd look ahead and say, 'What can we find to put in?' But people just don't worry about it now.

Chapter 14

Buttermilk and cabbage

"That's what keeps you healthy, girrl."

Madge, Heather and Merle reminisce with their mother about their greatgrandparents, grandmother and some of the characters at Trowutta when they were children.

Ruby

When Grandma Porteus first came to Trowutta she used to pick mushrooms and help wash up. And she used to make this lovely brown bread with a cup of bran and a bit of treacle in the water to mix it and a bit of melted butter. But she was only seventy-four then. She was sixty years married. Sometimes she'd go outside and pick rosemary off the bush and bring it in and boil it. She'd rinse her hair with it after she'd washed it, and she'd keep a little basin of it and when she combed her hair, she'd comb it through with this rosemary water.

Madge
I can't remember 'Old Gran', as we called her, ever doing any work. She sat in her black frock, in her apron and her cap, with her mittens, in this big chair, and she was the thorough lady. Or she thought she was.

Her Bible was always tucked into her chair and she'd read that Bible every afternoon, but we were not allowed to touch it. I often think how much we could have got out of it, or she could have imparted to us. But she didn't communicate with us like Gran Pacey did. She never even offered. Gran Pacey waited on her hand and foot. She used to get up, take them their tea and toast, go and milk her cow, come back and do the front room and have the fire ready when Old Gran got up. That was so as long as I can remember. We all as children really held her in awe. We respected her, but she didn't have the same tolerance with young people and the understanding Gran Pacey had. Gran we loved, but Grandma Porteus we just respected. She was so much part of our life even so, but such a contrast.

Old Grandfather Porteus was the sweetest old man. He liked a drop of whisky and Grandma disapproved. And she'd go looking for his bottle. Of course we knew where he kept it. He kept it under the potatoes in the shed. She'd say, 'Come with me, child', very broad, and away we'd go with her. And she'd poke about in the ferns and bushes, and swish around with her stick. But she never found it.

We knew, because he used to go out and sit on the potatoes. They'd be 'shot' – put all out then covered with bags, so they wouldn't breathe, and hidden under them would be the bottle of whisky. And his old mate, Tom Ryan, used to go out there and sit on a cold day, and they'd have their drop of whisky. Gran Pacey always saw that he had that little drop of whisky, but she wouldn't let him have a lot. She'd only leave a drop in the bottle.

Gran Emily Sophia Pacey, c. late 1930s

Heather
At the end of the verandah there was a little closed-in piece. They called it 'the flower house' and us kids were never allowed in. But we used to sneak in. We always thought he had a hide-out there too. He used to grow his own tobacco in a pot in the flower house. It was a lovely looking plant. Then he'd bring it inside and hang it from the ceiling to dry out. His pots were made from kerosene cans cut off, rolled in fancy ways. In fact they were the wash-up dishes. They used to have them cut cornerways and they'd wash up in one side and drain in the other, two triangles, opened out.

Grandfather Porteus was a small man. When he got older we always used to think he was like an Irish leprechaun, because he was just so little and wiry and bony, and had sharp features. He was lovely. With his Irish accent he'd always say, 'Oh Merril, me gerril'. He used to sing *The Mountains of Mourne*. He had a good voice when he was younger and he kept on singing when he was old.

Once he and Tom Ryan got in the shed, and old Tom had been to Smithton on his horse and brought back this bottle of whisky, and they must have consumed nearly all of it. In they came and Grandma had visitors! Someone from away, and she was putting on airs, being the real lady. And Grandpa came in and he was dancing! She drew herself up and she was so haughty! And this little fellow dances round and he chucks her under the chin. 'Whoosht, woman', he says.

The big china teapot with a beautiful velvet patchwork cosy was always on the hob all day. And Grandfather would come in and he'd have a drink. He'd put easily a dessertspoon, perhaps two if you didn't watch him, into his cup and then he'd drink the tea and eat the sugar. He had such sweet tea it was almost syrupy. But the kiddies used to climb up on his knee from very tiny, and he'd feed them this tea off his saucer and they'd be licking their chops. They thought it was wonderful. If somebody came in crying he'd say, 'What ails the child?' And he'd sit the kid on the floor with a sugar basin. That's how he cured all ills.

Madge

Old Gran was very fond of buttermilk. Gran Pacey used to milk the cow and she used to churn out in the little back porch. The buttermilk was always saved and put in this bucket, a black iron enamel lined bucket, the sort miners used to grind ore to test the metal. It was about a foot high and stood on a cupboard with a piece of cretonne round it where the pots were kept. Whenever we churned and were going down to Gran's, we took Old Gran her buttermilk. And whenever Auntie Pearl churned, she took buttermilk. So Old Gran always had it there.

And of course it soured and thickened as time went on. It'd go real curdy. There was a little dipper hanging on the side of the bucket, and she used to go and help herself. Every now and again she'd have a cup of this awful gooey buttermilk. It was that thick, and the smell of it was vile. You could hear it going plop, plop, plop, as she poured it out.

Old home at Trowutta, c. 1920s

And she used to say, 'That's what keeps you healthy, girrl'. She would lick her lips and say, 'That was beautiful'. She always said that we should drink buttermilk every day, and she did.

But everyone loved Gran's hop beer. They were all supposed to be teetotallers, Dad and all, but they used to say, 'Isn't this good?' It was absolutely beautiful. But one glass'd make you dizzy.

Gran Pacey loved cold cabbage. They'd often make their dinner of cabbage with a little end of bacon cooked over an open fire in a big iron pot. They'd never cook cabbage with the lid on. And there'd be bacon fat rendered down and they'd put this in and keep stirring and stirring and stirring with a big wooden spoon. It was like the wooden ladle they used to stir the porridge. They'd keep stirring and poking at it while it cooked and put a bit of soda in it to keep the colour.

Heather
Gran always drained the cabbage through a rather unusual colander, which probably came from the West Coast too, a wire strainer with a rounded bottom. It mightn't even have been a colander in the first place. They always made use of everything. Nothing was thrown away. Their milk billies were always seven-pound golden syrup tins. Anyway, she always pressed every little drop of water out, pressing a saucer turned upside down on the cabbage. Then she'd turn it out into a dish and put pepper and butter into it.

Gran Pacey's house, c. 1980s

And that'd be their dinner, perhaps with a little bit of fat bacon, not very much, but very fat, served with this great big plate of the most delicious cabbage. It was dark green cabbage and the outside leaves were always cooked. Every little bit of it was cooked in this bacon water. If there was any left over, Gran Pacey would pick at it all the time. They saved the hard stalks that were in the middle of the dark green leaves, and made pickles out of them, cut up with onions.

Ruby
There's a family story about cabbage – Gran Pacey wouldn't have enjoyed this cabbage: Old Granny Porteus's sister, Auntie Maggie who played ghosts in the bog in Ireland, came out here to live with her son and daughter. And after her funeral they found all the love letters she'd got from her beaux in Ireland before she was married. But she'd married a reprobate in the end. He went through two or three fortunes. His father set him up twice. Either she left him or he left her, but he kidnapped their two boys, Jack and Freddie.

They hated their father. They were frightened of him. He used to go to their college – they were always at colleges, – and say, 'I wish to see my children examined in such and such'. So they'd bring them out and of course they could never do any good because they were terrified of him. And he'd say, 'Thrash them, thrash them, thrash it into them'.

They had to stay with their father in the holidays and he used to take away their clothes every night so they couldn't run away. He had a housekeeper. And all these big dishes of food would be put out on the sideboard in the dining room. Well, one day the boys were so wild with him, they peed in the cabbage before he came. And their father said, 'Have some cabbage, my boys. Very fine cabbage'. They wouldn't. But the father ate it!

Jack did run away in a pair of Freddie's trousers. It was a week before he got home to his mother, all through London, but he found her. And his father never got him back. Freddie became an actor and Queen Victoria gave him a diamond pin. He always had it pawned and whenever he'd go to take a big job, he'd have to get it out of pawn. He was like his father.

Madge
When I was about five years old I'd go and get the paper at five o'clock in the afternoon when the mail came in. It was *The Advocate* from Burnie. After tea they'd sit around and my grandmother, Gran Pacey, would read it aloud from start to finish. The whole lot would share it – Gran's brother, Uncle Jack, her mother and father, and the aunties. And she would read every word of it, every night, all the world affairs, and now and then they'd pause and comment on it and talk about what was happening in Ireland. We didn't get it till afterwards.

Heather remembers when Gran Pacey got a wireless
Uncle Charl sent it to her, about 1929 or 1930. It was a big box type that sat on the table, and it had a big speaker, a horn. And you got a terrific amount of static just when you wanted to hear something. When the cricket was on in England I used to go and sit at Gran's probably till four in the morning with Dad. We'd make cocoa twice through the evening and listen to the results.

Madge
Our Grandmother Pacey was a very well-educated woman. She'd learnt French and painting and music at school in Ireland. She always talked to the children as if they were people. We'd walk around the garden and talk, and if something wanted doing she always had a little quotation to fit it, perhaps from the Bible. She knew her Bible from end to end. And then she'd explain it to you. She'd sing to us any time we asked, and often of a night. *I'll Take You Home Again, Kathleen* was one of her favourites.

When we had dances in the hall Gran used to play for a lot of them. She used to play *Ring the Bell, Watchman* for the barn dances. She'd always get to the piano and start with that while she had a little think what she was going to play. It was always her opening, and I never hear it but I think of Gran, even now. She was very musical, very talented. Right up until she died the children just adored her. My Colleen used to sing when she was a little girl and Gran would sing with her. They used to sing *The Garden Where the Praties Grow* and all these Irish songs together, Gran with her Irish accent and this little piping three-year-old voice. They'd sit together in front of the fire and sing away.

Merle
Mum used to sing to us. We'd buy a sackful of windfall apples for two shillings, from Spreyton and it would be put on the train. When Dad went to Lodge she'd sing these very sad Irish songs. She'd be bawling and we'd be bawling. Then we'd each get this green apple and be sent to bed chewing in one another's ears, because there'd be three if not four of us in the bed.

When we were in the top place Dad used to go off for the mail and we'd all gather round the fire and Mum would sing to us. *We Parted On the Shore*, *The Midnight Express* and all those. Real music hall stuff. And Dad would come home and we'd all be bawling. He often used to sit outside because Madge couldn't sing when he was there.

Heather
We lived about three miles up the road from Gran Pacey and we often used to visit on a Sunday. It was always a great night out if we could stay. Sometimes we were allowed to sleep with Gran in the big bed. Other times she'd make up a bed on the couch for us. We'd get awfully sleepy just at the time Mum and Dad were going, so Old Gran would say, 'Put the child to bed'.

And out would come old Grandfather Porteus's nightshirt and we'd sleep in that. There were no pyjamas. He always had a nightshirt. If you ever caught a glimpse of him through the door in the morning before he got dressed you could see his long skinny legs and his little feet sticking out from under his nightshirt. We always loved to get a nightshirt to sleep in. One of Gran's nighties wouldn't have been nearly the same.

Ruby tells about her mother's garden at Trowutta
There was a holly tree and a big japonica and two rhododendrons. She planted a white rose on each side of the path. And she had the

ordinary old gladdies that used to be all red in the early days. They'd be out in the summertime. The front was just glorious in the springtime because the trees were coming into bloom and she had yellow pokers which would be beginning to fade at the end of winter, but the daffodils were coming out. And it was just like a yellow light. She had an arch halfway down the path with a real passionfruit vine. It had beautiful flowers but never any fruit. She had gooseberries and raspberries and apple trees. Colin used to go and prune them for her. But they never did very well. They weren't worth bottling. Apples and all sorts of plums and Kentish cherries grew beautifully down in Edith, but up in Trowutta they just didn't do so well. The myrtle ground had no clay subsoil. Down at Edith Creek they had clay subsoil which held all the moisture better and was very good for fruit trees.

Grandfather kept bees. He always had a few swarms. They have a lot of bees in the district now, but they take them out to the bush, out to the leatherwood for certain seasons of the year. Where there's a lot of blackberries, you get blackberry honey. Some people like it but I think it's just tasteless. We were used to the real leatherwood.

Everyone that could come, came for Grandma and Grandpa Porteus's Diamond Wedding in 1926. We had it in the Trowutta hall at night. There was the family in the daytime. By that time the house had grown a verandah at the front and one side. And they built a wall of gum boughs and man fern fronds to enclose it. That was where they had the tables for the wedding breakfast. It was a nice day and they took some photos. I was standing on a stool behind Granny and Grandfather and I fell just as the man was taking it. Col was behind me and he held me up.

All the family from the West Coast and Hobart and everywhere, they all had to be put up. I built a bed, a timber frame, with chaff and potato bags for a base, and a kapok tick on top. And we got four kids into that.

Heather
Mum had to cook the sucking-pig. It was killed on Auntie Syl's property next door. I'd be just barely seven, Madge would be nine, Minnie would be ten and we were sent up to get this sucking-pig to take home to be cooked in the big Peters oven.

Auntie Syl gave it to us wrapped in a piece of newspaper, but of course it was too heavy for any one of us. So we threw the paper away and took a leg each and started carrying it. But that was a bit awkward, so Min said, 'Give it to me'. And she put it round her neck and carried it like a scarf. When we landed home she had hold of the front legs and the hind legs and the pig round her neck. And that's how we got it down there.

You cooked the whole thing and with a potato in its mouth. Mum had a huge baking dish, a great big black one, as black as your hat. It had come from Ireland. The pig was hanging out either end of that, head and all. But it fitted into the oven.

Madge
We were a very close family and had a lot of family sayings. We did a lot of visiting with one another and the greeting was always, 'Is the kettle boiling?' Joe Whelan once said of us, 'They know how to live, don't they?'

Mum and Auntie Syl always used to say to us, 'Tell the truth and there'll be nothing said to you'.

Auntie Pearl and Auntie Syl and Mum used to sit around the fire with their heads together talking and drinking tea out of the big cups with the gold shamrocks in the bottom. And they'd see us kids coming and stop talking and just say 'Ta polla richa', which means 'Little pigs have big ears'. They didn't tell us kids the juicy bits of family history. Mum kept very close-lipped about it. She didn't think it was suitable for four little girls.

My Grandmother Porteus had a long dining table with a green cloth to the floor. And she used to say, 'The Porteus men were a lot of villains and they used to hide behind the cloth'. And I always used to imagine these little men peeping out from under the tablecloth. It was a long time till I found out what she really meant about them being clergymen in the Church of England!

Merle
Whatever happened Auntie Syl would always say, 'It's all good tuition'. Everything taught you a lesson. If her scones were a bit black, she'd never let on that she burnt them, she'd always say, 'That's the way we like it'. We always were taught to make the best of things. And Auntie Syl used to say, 'You'd better keep me alive. I've spent my burying money'.

Heather
Gran Pacey used to say to me, 'This is me final flutter, Hedder'. There were lots of Irish sayings, but I don't know how to spell them. If you

were really hungry you'd say, 'I've got a fargurtha'. But we can't put the Irish brogue into it, like the old people did. There was one for 'Give me a kiss, you pretty girl', and one for 'The best child in the house'. And if you didn't know a word or how to pronounce it you'd say, 'pig's tit' or 'man on horseback'.

Old Tom Ryan had two great big banners which said *Cead Mile Failte*, 'A hundred thousand welcomes'. It was an old Irish greeting. And they used to hang them up at Brydges' place in the early days whenever there was a big get-together there. We had the first football matches and sports there and they built this big canvas and bough shelter where they had all the food, 'Kay mella fulcha', they used to say. Gran Pacey always used the Gaelic word *Ceilidh*. She used it for a Sunday gathering, a come-together of the family for talk and gossip, or a cosy chat with a friend. She used to say, 'It was a wonderful *ceilidh*'.

Ruby
Everybody took a bottle of jam when they went visiting. We had a neighbour, she was a dear. One day she wanted to give us a jar of her jam. She was looking in her cupboard for something particular, but couldn't find it. So she pulled out a jar and said, 'Whatever it is, it'll be nice'. So that's one of our sayings now too. Ted Sawley, Syl's husband, and Cliff Frost, Pearl's husband, used to call us 'Love', 'Duck' and 'Pet'. I was 'Love', Auntie Syl was 'Duck' and Auntie Pearl was 'Pet'. And Ted'd ring up and say to Pearl, 'Is that you, Pet?' And he'd be taking off Syl or me. Oh Ted, he was a funny man. He'd take off our conversations.

Heather
Mum always says, if something goes wrong, 'Well it makes a good story, anyway'. Or else, when things don't work out, 'That's as far as you go for ninepence'.

Ruby
When one of Madge's daughters was married, I was put with the bridegroom's uncle from New Zealand, and people at the table wanted me to tell this fellow the story of my wedding. Well, I didn't tell him much. I'd just told him a little bit and he got up and said, 'Well, you tell a good story anyway'. He didn't believe a word. He thought I made it up!

Like the English fellow that got sick of the Australian telling tales about snaring wallabies in the closed season and said, 'Bugger the wallabies!' So the Australian said, 'Well, bugger the Queen'. And that's what I thought about him!

We learnt a lot of rhymes at school to teach us things. 'Will you have some more?' she said. And he said, 'I've had sufficient'. I forget what went after that. That's why I said I get as far as I can go for ninepence. Another was:

> A brook and a little tree once went to school,
> To a bullfrog who lived in a pool.
> Of nouns and pronouns they soon had enough,
> Prepositions they found most unbearable stuff.
> 'I declare,' said the tree, 'I will not learn a thing'.
> 'You mean "Shall not",' retorted the brook with a fling.
> 'Shall' said the brook, 'Will' said the tree.
> Neither one knew enough grammar to see.
> Well, that tree is a willow wherever it grows
> And that brook is a shallow wherever it flows.

Pearlie had a great sense of humour – even when she got caught by her bloomers on the picket fence at Sawleys'! She was hanging over the fence and she said 'I got caught by the jawbone of me ass'. When Granny Paul came to stay with us and Pearl and I were milking the cows while Colin worked at the sawmill, all day long Granny Paul and Pearl would make little verses at each other. Granny Paul loved Pearl. She had a lot of funny sayings. When we were playing cards and you took a trick from her, Pearl'd say, 'You'd steal a worm from a blind hen'. Or she'd say to you, 'You're sitting there like a bird on a biscuit tin'. Or 'You're sitting there like a maggot looking down a marrow bone'. 'Drink's a curse. Down with it!' was another saying. And they'd hold their glasses up and swallow it!

Heather

One of Gran Pacey's sayings was 'There's always room for one more'. It was Mum's too. Nobody was ever turned away. We'd always find an extra meal or make up a bed somehow. Many's the pot of potatoes I've peeled to feed extras. But to make the meat go round we'd have to 'Tom Inneser', that meant we'd carve it very thinly. Tom was a mean sort of fellow. My mother had some funny sayings. Some were not very complimentary, like 'She had a tongue like a beggar's clap dish'. And she'd talk about being 'as funny as a piece of string', and 'as mad as a hoe'.

Uncle Charl would say 'You're not as silly as you are'. There's hardly a day goes by without we don't say something Charl used to say or do. He was a real character. Everybody loved him.

And Auntie Phyllis would say, 'If you have two loaves of bread, sell one and buy a lily'. That was just how she was. She loved beautiful things and didn't care much for practicalities. Even in the later years of her life when diabetes had affected her eyes and we took her out to the bush with an English friend, she raved on about the beautiful gum trees and said, 'I can't see it myself, but I know they're there'.

And cousin Minnie always says, 'There's nothing lost that a friend gets'.

There was an old Irishman, Connie Brouder, the one that said, 'Tell me, Micky, are you killed?' – he always grew strawberries. And if Dad had to go over, we'd go too, and he'd sit us up to strawberries and cream. In later years he made wine out of anything that would make wine, but he always called it his parsnip wine. One night some of the young fellows were drinking it and saying 'You can really taste the parsnip'. And Connie was chuckling next day. He said, 'It never saw a parsnip. It was made out of potato peelings and I strained it through the tail of my flannel shirt'. But he did grow parsnips specially every year. He'd sow one seed at a time, and they'd grow that big and round and long. He was famous for his wine. One day he'd been picking gooseberries and we came for some. And he'd had gout, so he'd cut the whole front out of his boot and his sock was piled high with buzzies, six inches high.

Poor old Burley Butler – he and his brother Harry went to the war and Burley lost an arm. He'd never accept a pension, he just kept himself, farmed, milked a few cows, mind you, with one arm. He was doing some blacksmithing one day and Uncle Tom Hancock was there with him. Tom said, 'I could smell this funny smell, and wondered what it was. And blow me, all of a sudden, old Burley started to dance and swear!' And swear he could! Tom said, 'I could see smoke and there was a singed patch of whiskers and a hole in his flannel shirt. From a spark from the furnace'.

Poor old Burley used to have bullocks and he got whooping cough. And he'd cough and he'd cough until he absolutely lost his breath. When he got it back he'd swear and that would make him cough again. He was a good mile away from where we lived, but on a cold, frosty morning us kids could hear him from the verandah. He'd be rounding up the bullocks and swearing at them. Then he'd have to stop and cough, and one would tread on his toe and he'd have another swear. It was as good as a circus!

Ruby
Poor old Burley. He was a good old fellow really, a real good type. When he came home from the war he was determined to make his living, so he took a contract carting the cream. A can of cream is heavy, so he took a couple of cans down to Spinks Creek and filled them with water to see how he'd handle them onto the cart. They gave him an arm with a hook on, but the only time he ever used it was to help him lift the cream cans onto the cart.

Madge
We got used to seeing that stump hanging out. He was always asking for a meal and he'd sit and yarn and move it all with his one hand. We weren't repulsed by it. I think it was Mum and Dad's attitude to him.

Ruby
There was another old fellow and his name – well, I do know, but I won't tell. We used to call him the 'skedjidoodle' man. He was the one who didn't put anything in the show because he didn't have a 'skedjidoodle' – a schedule. He was the fellow that said before a funeral that her entrails should be engraved on the coffin. Her initials, he meant! 'H'appendicitis', he used to say. 'H'it's caused by a h'air. But I don't know whether it's a h'air out of the h'atmosphere or an 'air out of 'is 'ead'. He sent Jack Frost over to the shop for h'ink and h'envelopes. So Jack said, 'H'ink and h'envelopes, h'ink and h'envelopes' all the way.

There was another fellow who batched with three or four others and he couldn't find a cup for himself. 'Well,' he said, 'I see all the cups are in vacancy'. He used to say that all the mulch on the ground made very good humorous.

Just after Joey Lyons, the politician, who came from Stanley, changed to United Australia Party from being a Labor minister, the inspector came to the Trowutta school. When he said, 'What's Joey Lyons now?' young Molly Finnegan put her hand up, and said, 'Please, Sir, a twister'.

A woman who grew vegetables would take the money on a Sunday, but wouldn't give you the cabbage. You'd have to come for that on Monday! That same woman sold eggs. I rang her up one day and asked, 'Can I have half a dozen?' 'Oh yes', she said. 'I've just brought a double-yolker in,' she said, 'and I'll send you that too'. So she sent it along and charged me for half a dozen. And when I opened up the parcel she'd given me five eggs because one was double-yolked!

Ruby of Trowutta

cylinder record player

wireless (radio)

Chapter 15

The Post Office

"Number, please."

Ruby and Heather discuss their work at the post office.

Ruby

We took the post office over from Mrs Frost, Pearl's mother-in-law, on 1 May 1930. In all the upheaval and bustle Lilian's birthday was forgotten. And Heather always says she grew up overnight. The post office was in a corner of the back porch behind the kitchen. The shop was at the other end behind the second bedroom. And the butcher's shop was behind the house. We'd been there just ten years when Col died on 6 May 1940, and I stayed till 1971. We added an extension to the side for the shop and post office in the forties.

Heather loved the work all the time she was doing it at Trowutta and then at Lileah after she was married. The post office was the nerve centre of the district, very important in people's lives. It didn't matter what people wanted, they had to get you first. And we were very glad to be there sometimes, to be able to help. People didn't all have phones then and they'd get us to ring somewhere for them. Or they'd send a message and transfer calls on to us. When they were growing potatoes and the crop was ready to go, you'd ring the merchants and they'd have to transport them. We rang Bishops, the carters, for several people. And once old Bishop charged the carting to the station to us instead of to Paddy Keenan. Orders often got charged to us from

Trowutta post office and house, March 1984, after Ruby Paul had sold it

the chemist in Smithton, because we'd put the call through for stuff for somebody.

Heather
When we first went there we had one line between four post offices – Edith Creek, Roger River, Irishtown and Trowutta. We all had our own signal and the phone would ring and you got so used to it you wouldn't hear it unless it was your own signal. Ours was three short rings. Roger River's was a long and a short. A cousin of ours was at Edith Creek and the girls on the exchange would never know which of us was speaking. In the finish they said, 'Are you people all related?' Mostly you see, you can easily pick up voices when you are working with them all the time.

First thing of a morning you'd ring all your faults through, line faults and phone faults. Smithton was our base and the mechanics would come from there. They thought we didn't know what was going on, but we did. They laughed about it afterwards. They'd say, 'We'll go to Mengha and Alcomie first and when we get to Lileah, it'll be nearly morning tea time'. After I married Murray I had the Lileah post office. But many a time if I was busy on the switchboard the boys would go in and make the cup of tea for me. Then they'd go back and do Irishtown and have lunch, then they'd go out and do Edith Creek and Roger River and get to Trowutta at afternoon tea time. They knew Mum always had an open house too.

To get through to other offices you had to go through the exchange at Smithton. They'd give you a line but you had to wait until it was clear before you could get your call through. Sometimes you'd be waiting three quarters of an hour for the line. That was nothing. And then you'd start and check what times other people have had their calls.

The Post Office

If you got the line you just sat on it and waited. A woman said to Mum, 'Mrs Paul, you're not supposed to have the line more than twenty minutes and you've had it for an hour'.

But it wasn't that long before we had a couple of lines each and we kept getting bigger switchboards.

The last one Mum had was a beauty. It was like a big organ. We used to keep it polished up and the inspectors would be that tickled about it. We had a big long passage where the phones were. It was cold and terribly tiring. When I left school and began helping I'd be standing at the phone in that cold passage, and used to get dreadful black and blue chilblains four inches across right up to my knees. The first switchboard was only about eighteen inches wide and high, and the plugs were on cords with pulleys underneath, hanging from the bottom. The holes for them were in a triangle, all numbered. The ones in the wall were too high. You couldn't sit. You'd stand by the hour trying to get your calls through. But we finished up with this lovely big board on the floor, like a sideboard, and a beautiful swivel chair they gave us.

When we answered we were supposed to just go on and say, 'Number please?' Or 'Identify yourself – your post office'. Or if it was a trunk call you would just go on and say, 'Trowutta'. You'd have so many calls banked up, you'd try to put them on one after the other, trying to get them through. They were only three minute calls, but some people wouldn't mind if you extended them. The number of calls a day varied with the time of the year, with the seasons. And it varied from the early days we were there until we finished up. Probably thirty to forty trunk calls a day. Just the ordinary everyday things you took in your stride, but it was surprising how often you got a call overseas or something a bit unusual.

There was one thing Dad always insisted. If we ever took a message for anybody, we wrote it down before we left the phone. The phone was just outside the kitchen with pencil and paper always there. Dad could hear me take a message, and he'd always say, before I even went into the kitchen, 'Did you write that down?' Because you'd be taking lots and lots of different messages from people that didn't have phones.

You handled a terrible lot of people's business. But everything was handled very secretly. Pensions and all those things, you didn't talk about. Phone messages and telegrams – everything was very confidential. Before they'd register you, before you were allowed to work in the post office, you had to swear to secrecy. And anybody that worked for you had to register. Mum had five or more girls working for her at one time or another after I married.

You had a book with all these codes. There was a lot of those. You'd get an official telegram all in code and you'd have to decode it. And sometimes you'd have to reply in code. You got used to it. You'd write out a telegram and often had to deliver it if we felt it was urgent. We wouldn't wait until mail time. I'd walk in the early days, later I had access to a bike. I was never that good on a horse. Of course later when everyone had phones on, we could ring them up and give it over the phone.

You had to time every call and write out a docket for each one – not from one Trowutta subscriber to another, but for what are local calls now, all Circular Head, Smithton and Stanley. We had piles of these dockets. Then we had to do all the accounting as well. You'd do your dockets up every day, or we usually did ours up once a week. Then at the end of the month we had to finish them all up. You'd add vertically and horizontally and put your totals down and everything had to agree. Sometimes you'd be tuppence or threepence out. It was no use putting it in or pretending it was there. You had to show it.

It was no good sitting to do your returns in the daytime because you'd get too many interruptions. So you'd be doing them after you'd finished your work at night. It'd be late and then you'd have a mistake and you'd go over and over it. So you'd just drop your pencil and go to bed and get up next morning and go through it and you'd find it straightaway. It'd happen time and time again. Then at the end of the month you had to get all your monthly returns away for your telegrams and all the money you'd handled. Dad used to do a lot of the dockets up. That was only when we first started. We knew nothing about it then.

Ruby
The exchange was open from Monday to Friday and Saturday morning. I used to do an hour on Sunday. In the end I had forty-nine subscribers and I was frightened I'd get the other one, because when you had fifty you had to have a continuous service. By then we had four trunk lines. And I was open from eight in the morning till ten at night. During the war after Heather married, I'd have a whole day's

washing up to do at night. We could close for an hour at dinner time. We could please ourselves, but if we stayed open we were doing it free. So I said, 'I think we'll have our dinner hour'.

I used to get called out by the cream carter in the night. He'd be held up with breakdowns. They used to cart the cream at night and they'd go out early and take two loads into the Duck River factory at Smithton. Then they'd go round Nabageena and get a load. And another lorry would go further up Trowutta and they'd go round Roger and Edith after. Then they'd put that all onto one lorry and they always did it right in front of our place. There'd be all these cans, bang bang bang in the middle of the night.

Heather
At Lileah we always closed at one o'clock on Saturday, then straight to football. It was a wild rush to get dinner over in the football season. It was a scramble but I always washed up the dinner dishes. I could never bear to leave them. I could always think up to Saturday dinnertime and then I went flat after that. It was hectic to try and live a normal life as well as doing the work and keeping your house. When they gave us the option of working extra hours, I opened at seven in the morning because we felt that was more beneficial to the farmers. But it was a long day from seven in the morning to eight at night. And then when you shut your door that was when your work started. Lots of times that's when you did your housework. We used to shut our front door at dinner time and that was when I put my washing on the line.

Ruby
The mail came six days a week. Before we came down to the post office to live we used to go out with Dad and wait until the bus came with the mail. When the post office was first opened they used to do up mail in bags for all along the line. It used to come on the train and the bags were put off at all the stations. When Pearl's mother-in-law had the post office, Cliff, Pearl's husband, used to go to the station every night in his car.

Cars used to have a running board like a step and I remember once coming up the Trowutta Hill with Cliff one night in his great big Buick car when its lights went out. It was pitch dark and freezing cold and I had to stand on the running board and hold a torch for him all the way through. That was the worst ride I ever had. It was a terrible night and the train was late.

By the time we got down to the post office the mail always came from Smithton by bus, an old white service car driven by Jack Vincent.

Jack and his wife boarded at the Frosts' and he used to bring the mail. The mail was due at about half past seven then. And we'd watch for it. From the back door at Trowutta we would see a car light coming out of Lileah along the top ridge, just a fleeting light, just for a few chain before it went down Beattie's Hill and we'd say, 'That'll be the service car now'. We could see it at ten miles away, and we'd say, 'Well, we've got nearly an hour to do things before the bus comes'. It had to go down through Nabageena and then Edith Creek, Roger River and then up to Trowutta.

The mail bags were sealed all the way along. And each post office had its own seal. At first we used to do them with sealing wax. You'd melt it as it went on and you'd put a lead seal on it. And you sealed it over a string knot. And you had a tool like pliers and you'd squeeze it together. It was fairly thick string. Very strong.

Heather
There was two grades of string. One was to tie up the letters in bundles. You'd sort your letters. During the war we got an official letter asking us to economise with sealing wax and string and to re-use all the official envelopes and forms. We must have been very conscientious. Sometimes you'd tie up a bundle of letters and it would have three knots in the string. We used to get sealing wax in bars about six inches long and half an inch wide. And when they'd get down so small that you couldn't hold them while they melted, I used to want to throw them away. But I was never let. Dad melted up all the little pieces in a Lucky Hit tobacco tin with the Union Jack on the lid, and poured the wax into some sort of a mould to make it into a little stick, so that we could use every bit.

All we were expected to do for the war effort! We had to save all the lead seals off the mail bags and send them in when we got a big envelope full. Once they sent them back because the strings weren't cut short enough! Dad was very strict about the lead seals, and pins and paper clips. If he ever found one in the sweepings, you know! At first they used to send a supply every six months, but then they brought in that we had to requisition.

Ruby
What I hated worse than anything was doing up parcels and soldiers' parcels. You had to have a list of what was in them and very often they'd been sewn up in canvas or hessian. And we had to open them, make the list and sew them up again before we sent it away. There was one lady who was a terror. She used to send parcels to New Guinea, to

the church. It was difficult to find out how much to charge to send them to different places too. I suppose I was a bit 'stoopid'!

Heather
Most of the time we were in the post office we only had to send a bag to Smithton and all our mail was resorted there. But we used to sort our mail into bundles. The coast, interstate and the local would all be in different bundles and we'd do one bag. The bags were very heavy canvas, about four feet by two feet. You'd never have too much to fit into your bag. Coming on Christmas we had to send two bags, but it was parcels. The registered bag went inside the other and it was a heavy red canvas, just a little bag, about a foot long and eight inches wide. Registered tended to make quite a bit of work, because you had to send this special bag and put it on your mail advice, as well as putting a special advice inside the bag.

You always had to put a mail advice in the mail to say what you were sending. Not how many letters, but how many parcels, registered parcels, certified mail. Everything was done in duplicate. All your records had to be kept at least two years and then about once in twelve months you'd go through and discard the old stuff. But every telephone docket, all your past mailman's receipt books. When the mailman brought the mail you had to sign for the bag and leave that paper with the bag. The mail would go out in the morning and come in at night.

At first it used to go out about quarter to seven, then later the time schedule was changed and it didn't go out till eight o'clock. And it used to come in about 5.30, then you'd be very busy sorting for an hour or so. Sometimes if it got a bit late everybody would all come in and have a cup of tea before they went home, sitting on the long bench at the back of the kitchen table. You'd have to try to get your tea started before the mail came in and hopefully it'd still be all in one piece by the time you were finished. There was no electricity, so you couldn't adjust anything.

People would have their tea and then come out for the mail. That's when everybody would see everybody. Then they'd want things in the shop. A lot of young fellows used to come and play quoits. They'd do it in the shop and they'd buy a cake of chocolate or cigarettes or lollies and they'd play for that. Bang, bang, bang, time and time again you'd hear the quoits thudding. They had a big board against the wall so that if they missed the peg they'd hit it. We used to play, we weren't too bad ourselves. I've still got those quoits and we play with them at picnics. There were a lot of young fellows around and five or six of them used to go over to Gran Pacey's, because she had a wireless.

Ruby
To run the post office we were given twenty-six pounds. That was our allotment. That was for stamps and postal notes. Our supply was four of everything. We weren't a money order office. You had to keep up your stock and keep up your change. They didn't mind doing one order a week but they didn't like you sending in twice. But if you ran short you had to get more. We had a cash box and a postal note book and a stamp book, and they used to be kept in the bottom of the cash drawer. Overall there was always twenty six pounds' worth. It went up as things got a bit dearer. It got that we could only buy two one-pound postal notes and there was 15/-, 10/-, 5/-, 2/-, 3/- and 4/-. There was 2/6 too. We had to keep a lot of them. And you had to keep a record of all of them.

We had one regular order and that was done up on Sunday night to go early on Monday morning and we'd get it Tuesday night. Then if you ran short towards the end of the week you would have to send another requisition. The official post office we had to send to, didn't like that because they were busy and they allotted one day a week to do up the requisition orders. And you sent your requisition for all the money you needed to pay your pensions and your endowment. That had to be sent a couple of days before and it'd come the night before pension day. We used to do our pensions regularly on the Sunday night and when she left school that was Heather's job after tea. Before that Dad used to do it. We paid all the pensions, all the military money.

There were some people who couldn't read or write much, so I always fixed up their papers and helped with their money. Some old fellows wouldn't transfer their pensions from here even after they left the district, so I still did them even though it was against the rules. One woman wouldn't transfer her endowment. She was too self-conscious to go anywhere else for it. So I fixed it up for her for years.

It was difficult trying to run a business in a post office in the war years. We had the shop and the petrol bowsers. We were issuing the ration tickets and petrol coupons and everything had to balance. Once we lost a whole month of petrol ration tickets and we always reckoned somebody had taken them out of the office. So we just wrote and said, 'Well, they're not here and we can't do anything about it'. And they gave us another issue. But you had to be so careful checking them. To get more petrol we had to have tickets to correspond. In a 500-gallon tank of petrol you were allowed one or two gallons overrun, and that was all the extra you got.

People'd come for petrol and say, 'We'll send you the tickets'. Well, with some people we just wouldn't have that. But if you'd put the petrol in first, you couldn't do anything about it. I'm still owed some coupons. You were allowed quite a big ration of petrol to run a milking machine, because that was an essential service. And for log trucks. Murray had a commercial allowance because of the business, and one ticket a month for private use of his car.

It was the same with sugar and butter and tea. You had to have enough tickets to get your new supply. All these tiny little tickets were less than one centimetre square, and every one of them had to be pasted on a form. Everyone was wanting coupons for this and that. One woman didn't drink tea and didn't use sugar and she had nearly a whole book of coupons. And she sent them all back. She wouldn't give them away. Anybody else would've said, 'Well, here's a few coupons'. But she didn't.

We were official war observers and had to report anything unusual. We had a Jap plane over, we really did. It was very low and we saw the men sitting in it and the Jap markings on it. Young Col had learnt about it at high school, he knew the different kinds of planes. After we'd reported it they rang back shortly and we heard one voice say, 'Clear the line, it's of national importance'. This was when we had two or three on a line. They were trying to trace it, but not to make a fuss and frighten people. A couple of days later they rang and said, 'We traced the plane. We know what it was'. But we knew very well they didn't.

Heather
Every morning we had to give what was called 'the flash'. We did that at seven o'clock. They'd ring through and they'd want the wind, the clouds, and we had to check our times so that ours was exactly accurate with theirs. Time was very important if we had anything to report during the day.

There was a funny side too. A man brought in all these Christmas cards he'd received and wanted to reply to them. So he threw them all on the counter and said, 'Are they the ones I've got to send?' I said, 'Those are the ones you've just got'. He said, 'Yes, but I've got to send an answer'. I just counted them and said, 'Well, what sort do you want?' And he said, 'You pick them out'. So I picked them all out and then he said, 'Now, here are the addresses'. And he got me to write on all of them and address them, ten or twelve cards, about two hours work. There was the girl who had fifty-four Christmas cards. She sent them in with her brother-in-law and rang me and said, 'Len's got the money but I didn't like to ask him to stick the stamps on. There's fifty-four. Would you do them for me?'

The post office was at the back of the house and people used to come round and straight into the porch. Mud and all out of their swede paddocks all over our clean floor. There was one old fellow used to spit and Madge gave him both barrels one day for doing it, because she'd just finished scrubbing the floor. And I don't think he ever did it again. Mum thought it was a dreadful thing to do. Mum wouldn't have said it.

Ruby
The inspector 'd just come, and he'd go through all your books and all your money. And anything you wanted to know, they'd tell you. I used to like to see them, but they wouldn't let you know when they were coming. But we usually knew, because the girls'd ring us from Irishtown post office and say, 'He's on his way'. We knew what they meant and there was always a flurry to get the last speck of dust up. But he was a nice old chap, that Mr Kearns. They'd always count your money, even though it was only twenty-six pounds. To the last ha'penny they'd count it.

Heather
I never cared whether he came or not, because our books were always up to date. They had to be. You knew that if you were short in your money you didn't have enough to get your new supply. You used to count every penny, every ha'penny. People would bring them to pay for their stamps, so sometimes you'd get this great heap of pennies and ha'pennies. And you had to get rid of them, because there was no bank.

Chapter 16

Emergencies

"Somebody had to help them, didn't they?"

In emergencies people always turned first to the post office for help and so much depended on the postmistress. Ruby, Madge and Heather remember some of the dramas in the district when they had the post offices at Trowutta and Lileah.

Ruby

When you're at the post office there's no other help for everybody around. Often there was no roads and it was the only help they could get.

Madge

Mum always helped in emergencies. Many a time I've seen it dark and raining and Mum putting on a pair of boots and a long black coat and heading off either to deliver a baby or sit through the night with somebody. Gran Pacey used to do the same. When Gran no longer did it, Mum did. She had no training as a midwife, but lots of common sense. She'd walk – rain, hail, shine or in the dark, metal road or mud. Many a time Mum would come home and then go to work. Without having slept probably, or just having dozed in a chair beside a patient.

Heather

We were on call day and night. It was just part of your life. You had it on your mind all the time. From the time we went to the post office Mum and I both slept with our doors open. We never ever shut our bedroom doors. My slippers were always by the bed and the dressing gown on the end. If the phone rang in the night you knew it was trouble and you'd shoot out. Often you wouldn't even stop for your dressing gown and slippers. Somebody'd ring and they'd say, 'Help, we want help!' It might be an accident on the farm with a tractor or horses, or transport for somebody sick.

At Lileah, Murray'd go straight away while I'd organise other help. You'd only have to send out a call and help came from everywhere. Somebody would always make their car available. It was a wonderful community spirit, and it was the same in Trowutta. The night the Taylors' baby was born Mum went off on the back of a motorbike.

Ruby takes up the tale

George Porteus always came to the rescue and he had Mrs Stevens on the back and I was on the front. I'd jumped out of bed in a terrible hurry and I didn't wait to do up my coat. It was straight and a bit tight. It wasn't meant for motorbike riding. Anyway, you never saw such a slurry road as we had to go through on this night and into this great big pool George goes! Straight through. And I was wet up to the waist! When we got to the house the doctor was there and a nurse somebody had rung for. The doctor had an old pair of Blucher boots, no laces in them, and he took off his shoes and put them on. And the poor old nurse had lost the heel of her shoe in the mud.

Anyway, I didn't have to deliver that baby because the doctor arrived in time and he told me a story. He went to deliver a baby at one place where there were two little boys and he heard one say to the other, 'That bugger's got his little black bag and I bet he's got another bloody baby in it'. That was Dr Packham. Fancy him telling me that story!

I used to go and sit with a little old couple, Mr and Mrs Hall. He'd sit by the fire all night and as long as he was awake he'd be saying the Lord's Prayer. But he never got right through it. He'd start all over again. The doctor said the old lady had had a brainstorm and there was nothing he could do. What's a brainstorm? A stroke, I suppose. But of course somebody had to help them, didn't they?

There was always a doctor at Smithton. Colin went to see him once when he had a bad shoulder. The doctor said, 'Go in there and take your shirt off'. So he did and sat there shivering for about twenty minutes before the doctor came back. Col reckoned every time the doctor went out he'd take a sip at the whisky bottle. Eventually he came back and said, 'I'll tell you what to do. Give it a good rub with whisky'. So Colin said, 'All right, you drink and I'll rub'. And he put on his shirt and went out.

Heather
The night we came home from a card evening at Edith Creek at 12.30 or a bit later, just as we were getting into bed a call came, 'There's a shooting party down at Marrawah and one of the men has failed to return to camp. We want to leave at daylight with a search party. Would you organise it?' By half past four in the morning we had thirty men on our corner ready to leave. But the man was never seen again.

Ruby remembers another incident with a happier ending
There was one man lost in the bush from Nabageena and the whole district was out looking for him for a week. His father rang me the first day he was lost. He said he just went for a walk. He was a little bit slow and when he didn't come home his father looked till late in the night and said, 'We'll find him in the morning'. They looked all day themselves and couldn't find him, so they rang me.

I rang Heather first and then I rang around and I had thirty men on the road and Heather had about the same number. I rang the mill and the mill stopped and the men all came over, and all the farmers around. At night when the men would come out of the bush we were there at a sort of camp with kerosene tins of tea, boiled on a log fire, and sausage rolls and scones and sandwiches and cakes.

If anybody found him they were to fire so many shots. It was no use cooeeing, because nobody would know who it was. Six days he was lost and he came out on a logging track at the back of Lileah. One of Heather's neighbours found him and put him on the back of a motorbike and brought him to their place. He was wet and cold and filthy after being in the bush for a week, and she gave him brandy and sugar in hot water and he pulled such a face. Only recently something came up about it and somebody said, 'Then he walked out of the bush whistling and singing'. And I said, 'If you'd seen him when he arrived at Heather's you wouldn't have said he was whistling and singing'.

It was a fairly big family and he used to help about the house. It was always his job to clean the back porch. And when Heather rang to say he'd been found, his sister was cleaning up out the back and she just dropped the broom and fire shovel and came straight to get him to take him home. And when he walked in the back door he said,

'What's all this mess doing here?' That was the first thing he said! Because there was never a speck of dirt in the porch when he was doing it.

Heather
One day a woman rang and said, 'Will Murray come over? The children have set the barn alight and they're in it!' Murray didn't wait. He rushed over, tore down the back of the barn and got the two little boys out.

Another time a woman rang and said, 'Would you send help! The house is on fire!' In about two minutes flat I had tractors and bucket brigades coming from all directions. I just rang everybody and passed the message on. And we saved the house. The following week her husband was in the shop, talking about the fire, and he said, 'Now I know what to do when the house catches fire'. And everybody standing round said, 'Yes, Mac, what?' And he said, 'Ring Mrs Reid'.

All around us at Lileah were dairymen with big herds of cows. We had one cow and Murray just used to milk her wherever he caught up to her. He went out to milk her one day and she was in a waterhole with only her nose above the water. She was nearly drowned, and being on his own he couldn't get her out. So he rang for help and within a few minutes we had eight or ten men to help get Reid's cow out of the waterhole. Two tractors came and they put this rope around her and pulled her out. They thought she was dead, but she lifted her head and then they thought perhaps she'd be all right. So Murray mixed up this big jug of Sykes Drench. We used it a lot if there was a cow sick or a bit cold or pinched up. It was a great thing to have out in the country where there were no vets. Murray put about a half a cup of rum into it, to warm her up. He was in the kitchen stirring it up and it was all nice and hot and you could smell it. One of the farmers standing there waiting to help said, 'If the cow's dead when you get back, I'll drink it'.

Anyway they tucked her all up with bales of hay and said, 'We can't do any more than that with her'. Murray said, 'We'll light a fire around her in the morning if she's dead'.

But when he got up she was bellowing out in the garden. So it was either the rum or the hay that went all right. She came good. She never had another calf but we milked her for eight more years.

One of our neighbours at Lileah was a wonderful nurse and if anybody needed any medical assistance it was Mrs Young they sent for, because we were such a long way from the doctor. There was usually two doctors in Smithton. But even if you could contact them on the phone it would take a long time for them to get out here. And there was no ambulance station. The hospital was at Smithton too.

There were farm accidents. One man who tipped the tractor over on top of himself was killed and we had to get help. Then there were the fires. A lot of the houses were not very well insulated and a lot of the ceilings were timber, and what caused trouble was the birds that got in under the eaves and built their nests.

At one time there was a house burnt down at Trowutta and we could see the fire from our place. Dad went round and came back with the whole family to stay the night with us. I remember Dad bringing them in. The mother had the baby in her arms and she pulled the shawl up over her face, she was crying. There was a little boy and Mum had a family of girls and her only boy was a baby, so we had no pyjamas. So Mum took the elastic out of the legs of a pair of her bloomers so that they'd look like pyjamas and he was happy to go to bed in those. Mum would never be stumped.

You were the centre of everything, you had to organise it, but the response that you got was overwhelming. You'd be so much part of the district. It just shows you how much depended on the small post office and the postmistress.

Ruby of Trowutta

Chapter 17

The shop

*"It was hard work and no glamour attached to it ... I always said
I raised my children on the end of the counter."*

Ruby

Things were very bad soon after we took over the post office and the shop. It was in the Big Depression and people were very poor. We just had one change of clothes then. You wouldn't have any more. But we always had clothes for the children. The government gave interest-free loans for the farmers to pay the labourers, so we got enough to pay men that were out of work. You'd get a man for 25/- a week and he'd keep his family on that. We had to pay it back but we had a lot of time to pay it in small amounts over the years. I remember paying the last seven pound ten after my husband died.

On Saturday night they'd come in and spend what they'd earned during the week. There was one poor old fellow, he had seventeen children. And another one with a big family used to wonder if he could buy a packet of milk arrowroot biscuits to take home. It's so hard when you've got little children. I nearly sent Father broke because I used to give them things and not put them down. I thought they weren't getting paid enough, though it was really as much as we could afford. If we had men working for us they always got their potatoes and swedes. We always gave them things like that.

We were all right, though we had to take in a lot of things for debt, cattle, sheep or whatever people could give us. Several people owed us money. One man cut forty ton of firewood for us. We had the stove and the open fireplace, and they owed us a fair debt so they went into the bush and cut the wood to clear their grocery bill with us. Then a bushfire came and it was all burnt. Another time we took a very big sheep from a man. It was a very hot day and they put it in a spring cart and when they got it out it was dead. And that came off a bill.

But that was preferable to the dud cheques. We never got that many. Sometimes it would be accidental, he'd think he was all right. It would surprise you – some of the cheques that bounced, but most of them, they'd soon come good. Any of the farmers round about. What you had to watch was the travelling public, or those that only came and stayed for a little while and gave their cheque. The Trowutta people, if they couldn't pay you, you might have to wait a year, but they would pay you.

Heather
It was horrible if you accepted a cheque and then had it returned by the bank. You'd have to go and try and get it made good. It wasn't very pleasant and I had to do it from the time I left school, before I was fourteen. I wasn't always the most tactful person, but that was one of the lessons of life. It was a small community and everybody were friends. But they were not dealing with each other. It was because you were in business that you stood apart. They were dealing with you, you were dealing with them. And you'd be the only one in the district to know that that man hadn't paid his bills or had given you a dummy cheque. You were alone in that.

Our stores came in on the train and the carrier used to get them from the station and bring them to the shop. Goods used to come in lined boxes which weighed fifty-six pounds. Not much was ever in packets. You had to weigh most things. The dates came in slabs, cut in squares that just fitted the box exactly. You almost had to pull the box to pieces to get the slabs out and then you'd break them up. They were much nicer than the dates you get in packets. Currants and sultanas came in boxes too. Coconut was always in bulk. Dried fruits, apricots and peaches, would come in bulk. So did icing sugar. That'd get damp in the wintertime. It was sticky and difficult. Or else it'd go hard. People'd order it and we'd weigh it out. We never had anything weighed up ahead, because it'd go damp in the bags. It'd keep when left in bulk but not otherwise. It was impossible then to get fruit or self-raising flour in packets. But tea was always in packets. We never had bulk tea.

You'd cut your cheese on a block. But you'd get used to it. You could cut a pound of cheese within a fraction. As far back as I can remember Dad always bought his cheese from Montagu, a ten-pound cheese. He'd buy one to use and one to hang up to mature, and that would do us until the next cheese season. He was very fond of cheese. He used to eat cheese and apricot jam together. Cheese from the Montagu factory took prizes in London. Mum always had it in the shop until the factory closed years afterwards. We used to keep it in the shop at Lileah too, and we sent cheese as far as Hobart.

Ruby
And as sure as we got the cheese in, we'd get the mice and rats. They were in a lot of the early houses. But ours was supposed to be ratproof. We had a loose lining board, but as soon as I fixed that I didn't really have all that much bother. I used to have a cat. And we used to have cats about the shed. They kept the mice down. Colin used to feed them, he used to give them a little something with milk.

The cheeses were all right if you could keep them in a cupboard. I had two I used. One was my old dresser. I put the cheese on slats and kept it turned. It used to go fairly mouldy on the outside. But you had to be careful not to break the crust or they'd go that mouldy it'd go right through. I often used to have to cut into it as far as the crack went and wring a cloth out in vinegar and throw it over, to keep it from drying and cracking until it was gone. And I used to hang them up from the ceiling as well. When Colin was home he'd do it with a bit of looped binder twine round each end.

I only bought ten-pound cheeses. And people would come out from Smithton and want to buy the lot. And I wouldn't let them have it. Mr Graham, the agricultural man, he used to say, 'Why can't we take the lot?' I'd say, 'You can't have the lot'. Then perhaps he'd get another one next time he came. They were easy to get rid of.

We had a bin that held a bag of flour and a bag of sugar at one time and when the lid was shut they were quite safe. I didn't buy big bags. I used to buy sugar from the merchant and I used to get flour from another shop, one bag at a time.

The salt was the biggest problem we had in the shop. It'd get damp all round if you didn't have a container for it. We had sugar and flour bins but we never had anywhere to put our salt. We didn't always have a crock. Salt was always by the bag and if we didn't keep that in a stone crock it would melt. And if you spilled a little bit on any of your weights or your scales, in an hour it'd be all rusty and eat into everything. It was terrible stuff to handle. We used to keep about half a bag in the crock and the rest would be left in the bag until we had room for it. But your cream of tartar and soda and saltpetre, that was always kept in glass jars in the shop. We used to get great big glass jars with lollies in and they were great for keeping things in. They had big lids and they were very handy.

Heather

The biscuits used to come in big tins and you'd weigh them into paper bags. Sometimes you'd get a tin, and it'd come all the way on the train and there'd be a terrible lot of broken biscuits. We had a lot of waste with biscuits. Then we had to package up all the empty tins and send them back. They were so bulky and awkward to handle. You had to bind them together with twine, bound three ways across, twelve or sixteen to a bundle.
Big biscuit tins were almost two feet high and a foot square. Then there were smaller ones and you'd pack them up separately. You'd often sell biscuits by the tin. We used to get a very nice biscuit – banana creams. That was a very nice biscuit. Before we went to the shop Mum used to buy a tin of those as a treat for Christmas. We kids loved them.

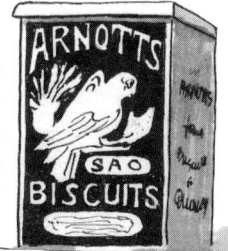

Rolled oats came in bags. There was a seven-pound bag. We sold a lot of those. We never bought rolled oats in bulk. In the 1940s when Murray and I had the shop at Lileah there was rolled oats in packets as well as bags. There were plenty of breakfast foods about then. They all came in packets, and macaroni and spaghetti came in packets.

Your bag costs were terrific. Plain bags, all brown paper, and the only white bags we'd get were the lolly bags, 8-oz and 4-oz lolly bags. Always tied with string, and break your string when you tied it. You'd never stop to cut it. You'd cross it one against the other and snap it. You can't break that nylon stuff now. When the travellers who brought the first samples of polythene wrapping came round, they told us it was going to be the greatest thing in wrapping but we couldn't see it at the time. They said, 'It will almost take the place of paper bags and wrapping paper', and we just wouldn't believe it. Then it wasn't very long before it proved itself and the travellers were right.

Ruby
The lollies were really lovely and you would be able to keep such a big variety, because even then the kids had money to spend and they'd come and we'd help them to choose their lollies. One woman used to spend all the endowment on lollies. She said, 'Well, that was for the children'.

It makes my mouth water now to think of those lovely big boxes of ha'penny novelties. Then they got to be a penny. There'd be an assortment of lollies. There was ha'penny and penny novelty boxes and oh! there was everything in them – licorice sticks and pink and white striped walking sticks and silver sammies – they were like a nougat stick coated with very thin chocolate, wrapped at one end in silver paper. Chocolate guns and bananas and gobstoppers and musk sticks, silver sticks and there was a coconut stick, pinky red and about eight inches long with coconut all over it. They used to look beautiful when you opened the box, all arranged, all fitted in, in their little groups. It was a lovely thing for a kid to have a ha'penny to spend. And he'd take that long to choose. While they gloated over this big box, that was when you got to know their mums and dads.

And there were sherbet sticks, sherbet bags with licorice. Lollies other than sticks came loose and we kept them in big glass bottles. Licorice allsorts, mint lumps and jubes and jellies. We used to get beautiful chocolates, chocolate gingers, and a round toffee with chocolate in the middle. There was Fantales and Tip Top toffees. And Columbines. We bought some in big glass bottles, but they were dear because we had to pay for the bottles.

We always had chocolate frogs, a penny each, and then they got to threepence. Sometimes they were wrapped in foil. The frogs were MacRobertson's, and the chocolate koalas were Cadbury's. And another thing we used to get at Eastertime, they called them hot cross buns, but they were chocolate with a big white cross on top. Heather used to have Easter bunnies and hot cross buns at Lileah, but Easter eggs came later. We never had Easter eggs. But we had conversation lollies. They were about when I was a kid. When we were growing up the boys and girls really used to use them. Not at school, you wouldn't look at a boy when I went to school.

Heather
The boiled lollies used to come in tins. We had to keep the lids on tight, otherwise they'd go sticky. There were satin ones and humbugs and aniseed balls. We used to sell aniseed balls eight a penny and that would give you ninety-six for a shilling. There was an old man who

used to come for his aniseed balls and he was giving me a bit of cheek about something so I said to him while I was counting them out, 'I'll give you two less for that'. He came back a couple of nights later. And he said, 'You told me you'd only given me ninety-four and that's all you did give me!' He'd gone home and counted them!

You'd make friends with the kiddies very quickly, because they identified you with their lolly supply, and they'd come in with grins on their faces. A little fellow came in at Lileah with a bunch of daisies and buttercups in his hot little hand and passed them over the counter to me with such a big grin. Then you'd see them gradually grow up, and most of them respected you. Some got a little bit big for their boots. We had a bit of trouble with one family. They'd knock at the window of the post office and ask for stamps and while you'd go and serve them there, another one would slip into the shop and help themselves. Several of them were doing it before we caught them.

At Lileah we were a grocer's shop that had everything you could think of. We kept a big range of stuff, from expensive stuff to the cheaper lines. We called it just a general store full-stop. My husband Murray had it first. He'd been in it with his stepmother and father. He was managing it, but they all did their share. We took it over from them when we were married in 1943 and we had it till 1965. When I went there, I said, 'We'll do it for ten years and get out'. Because I knew it was hard work, and by the time we were a family it wasn't easy. But it didn't turn out that way.

We had a store room next to the Lileah shop and we used to keep our cheese on a shelf up near the ceiling. A chap who lived right in the bush came in wanting some cheese. So I had to get one down off the top shelf and it was a bit high for me. I'd climbed onto the first rung of the stepladder and the cheese slipped and hit me on the bridge of the nose. I was sure I was going to black out. There I was in the store room and this chap was in the shop, and I thought, 'I musn't go out to it'.

I staggered back into the shop and he said, 'Are you all right?' I served him with the cheese and he went home and rang me up and said, 'Are you all right? Is Murray home yet?' He was very exact in everything he did, and everything he said. He used to hesitate when he went to tell you something, to make sure he was saying exactly the right thing. Once we delivered some groceries out to him and later he found sixpence on the ground where we had parked the car. So he rode his bike straight to the shop because he was sure that was our sixpence.

Some of the people were such characters, just so different, so individual. They were very, very good citizens. But then there were others who did not have any interest in the community or the district at all. They were just there for the season and they'd be gone, and it didn't matter to them anything that was going on. So those of us who worked together as a community were carrying the burden, and it was left to a few old stalwarts to take care of the things that mattered. That was in the post-war period when a lot of people moved about. There was full employment and plenty of money about and people would come in for a season, make quite good money and move out.

During the war it was very difficult because you just couldn't get your supplies through. There was no road transport. Everything had to come by rail. A lot of our stuff was packed in straw in big crates and we'd have to cart it from the rail, about six or seven miles down the road. People would come and stand around waiting for you to unpack your goods and see if any of the things in short supply were there, so they could grab them.

We were getting an issue of tobacco each month based on what we had been buying earlier and I remember trying to unpack these packets of tobacco with a handful of straw to camouflage them, so that I could get them under the counter. That way people who were not there got their fair share too. You had to do all sorts of things to be fair to everyone.

One man rang and said, 'If I can get some tobacco, I'll give you my weekly order this week'. He wasn't even a customer of ours and I was so upset. I said, 'What sort of a business do you think I'm running? What sort of a person do you think I am to give somebody else's cigarettes to you just to get one order?' It was a dreadful thing to ask me to do.

We had Law Somner seeds. They were in packets, sixpence a packet, we never bought any loose. We had toys and we had fancy goods. We had bread. We didn't have drapery or clothing, but we had a newsagency. We didn't have gum boots because the Co-op butter factory kept them. And we had lots of hardware – horseshoes and horseshoe nails and milking machine parts and veterinary supplies. And we had petrol. We always had candles and some lamps, but when the electricity came there was no need for lamps. We couldn't have frozen stuff till the early electricity days. It was hard work.

Ruby

When we'd get busy in the shop, one would always have to get up and run to the post office. There was no order in our lives then. The shop was always open. We used to close the post office on Saturday afternoon, but you'd still be busy in the shop. You couldn't refuse anybody if they came. We used to look forward to Saturday night's tea. We'd set the table and say grace, everything we used to do before we had the shop. Afterwards, with the shop, I'd be dishing the dinner and serving the kids, just to get it over and done with. It was rough and tumble, meals had to be done and got out of the way. That's what things were like and that's what you did.

We didn't even get Sunday to ourselves. But we always had a nice dinner. We'd have two big white table cloths a week, one on Wednesday and one on Sunday. Until we went to the post office and got so extra busy, a big carving set was always put on the table on Sundays, a knife, fork and steel, and Colin always carved the meat. And the vegetable dish was always put on the table and I served the vegetables.

Heather
At Lileah our girls always played hockey on a Saturday morning and sometimes one of us would have to take them. I never knew when I left on Saturday at dinnertime, what we were going to have for tea on Saturday night. Often we used to have what the girls called a picnic tea. It was the only time I didn't set the table. We'd light a good fire and just have what they wanted around the fire. Usually something on toast.

Ruby
Crumpets when crumpets came in. I remember the first crumpet I ever had. It was about 1938. We were playing cards with an old lady who was blind. Afterwards we sat round the fire and toasted crumpets for supper.

But you had to clean the shop. Everything had to be cleaned. As you filled your shelves, you'd keep the shelves treated. I had a dirty muddy road and the floor was just boards. I had a scrubbing brush that I put on a handle. I'd wet the floor and scrub it and the girl I had helping me would mop the water out and dry it patch by patch.

Heather
I did most of the store work. You would be piling cases of preserved fruit, two dozen large tins, holding them up over your head. It was heavy work and no glamour attached to it. You stacked your boxes up with the preserved fruits stacked up in piles, labels out so that you knew what they were. Then you'd have tins of fish and tins of vegetables. Crates and crates of sweets and big boxes of dried fruits,

and we'd be stacking them up one on top of the other. You'd have to lift them up and you'd have to lift them down. Sugar would be 70-pound bags and flour was 150-pound bags. And I had to empty them into the big pine bins. Later self-raising flour used to be in 25-pound and 7- and 2-pound bags. And there were cartons and cartons of breakfast cereals and they all had to be handled.

Ruby
That was what made me give up the shop in the end. I've had them piled up to the ceiling. I remember there was a case of self-raising flour in seven-pound bags half way up a wall and I said, 'This is the last time I'm going to do this'.

Heather
When I was at Lileah I preferred to have our children out with us in the shop. First they were in a cot at the back. Then I had a high chair I used to strap them in while I worked, and when they were older they would come and sit on one end of the counter while we were working and all the travellers knew them. I always said I reared my children on the end of the counter.

Service car. Back: Lilian, Ruby, Sylvia Sawley (nee Pacey), Pearlie Frost (nee Pacey). Front: Madge, Pat Frost, Colin (Ruby's son), Merle, Hector (driver), Jack Frost.

Chapter 18

The butcher shop

"I cut them up from the hoof to the horn."

Ruby, Heather and Madge reminisce about the butcher shop they ran and the first cars in the district.

Ruby

We had a butcher shop as well. And we killed our own meat. You'd kill a sheep and leave it overnight to cool. You'd have a bag that would hold it and cover it all over, and you'd hang it up in a tree. Up there it would keep a fortnight. When Dad was killing cattle he'd use an endless chain to haul the carcase of beef up to the ceiling of the slaughter house. When we killed for the shop it was in the slaughter-house and the carcase would be hung there to set overnight.

But you had to be very careful. Rats, possums, native cats, even just ordinary cats could come down and chew through the bag. So Dad got a great big iron disc, dome shaped, like a hood over the meat to cover it. And from the disc we had an endless chain fastened so that it couldn't slip. And you'd put it up whole. You had a gambrel and spreaders which went through the hind shanks. And you'd lower it with this chain and bring it inside onto a bench on the verandah or the kitchen table and cut it down through the backbone in halves.

We always sold the skins. The men would come round for the hides. They had to be salted. Dad always did that. He salted it with coarse salt, then folded it in a very special way so that the edges of the whole pelt were turned in, but the raw skin was never against the hair. Somehow he used to get all the edges turned in and the whole hide would be folded into a square perhaps two feet square. It was an art.

The bags were cotton. We had big enough to cover a bullock. Several dozen yards there were, it took a bag of ten widths of material to cover a bullock. Two of these huge meat bags would fill the copper. And they all had to be washed every week, soaked in cold salty water to get the blood out and boiled thoroughly next day to be ready for the following week. We had four of those big bags each week to do.

Col was sick for a long time, so I used to cut the whole thing up. I had two men who used to come and hold the carcase. They'd bring it into the slaughterhouse. Col had a wooden block, a piece out of a tree. It was too high for me, so they made me a box to stand on. And I could find every joint, cut every joint on a bullock, joints round the shin, and the leg where you cut the round steak, rump steak and the undercut, skirt steak and everything else. Beautiful shins of beef we used to have and we sold them for a shilling, and one and threepence for a clod. The clod was the front one, bigger than the back.

They said they thought I didn't know anything about meat, and I said, 'I cut them up from the hoof to the horn, so you can't tell me anything about it'. I knew where it came from. Col laughed about that.

The days were never long enough for all we had to do. We always had the cows to milk, no matter what else we had to do. And the casks of brine had to be made each week. We used to corn a leg of mutton. And we used to sell corned beef. It was beautiful corned beef, fourpence a pound. What they make the roll of now, we used to sell in flat pieces. We made our brine with coarse salt and saltpetre.

We had to clean these big wooden casks. When you washed them up you'd empty the brine and you'd have to start a fresh lot. We used to make a brick red-hot in the fire and scrubbed the casks with it, sterilise them with a hot brick in the water. I almost had to crawl into one to scrub it out. Even Heather couldn't do it. We'd bale them out with a bucket. They didn't have a bung. When we washed them, you had to tip it out on the floor. It was a concrete floor and it drained to one corner.

Heather

When Dad was delivering meat he had a bus specially built for him, a butcher's bus, with a place to hang his scales and perforated wire sections round the top for air. It was lined with varnished timber and could be set up just like a butcher's shop. And that used to have to be scrubbed with sandsoap in and out.

You had to get inside and you couldn't stand up to do it because it wasn't big enough, so you crawled in. The roof had to be scrubbed inside, with the water running down your arm, down your elbow, because you were scrubbing it up above your head. And he had four pine boxes and they used to have to be scrubbed with sandsoap before they were loaded up each morning. And Dad always carried a cloth and a towel. Always before he started serving, he'd wash his hands. He wouldn't go near the meat until he'd washed his hands.

Mum used to render all the fat and strain the dripping in the big black meat dish, this huge black meat dish we keep talking about, that came from Ireland. We'd cut up all the suet and the caul fat fairly fine and put it in the oven, and then as the fat came out we'd tip it into basins in big trays. When they were set they held just a pound. Then we'd turn them out and if there was any sediment we'd scrape it off. Such a lot of work and it was sixpence a pound for that. All these basins had to be washed. And we didn't even have a tap. You had to go out to the tank, fill the kettle, carry the water in the kerosene tin and put it on the fire for your washing up. It wasn't just now and again, but a regular thing.

When we got very busy, we'd have a fair fire on and we'd put this big dish of fat in the oven to render and it'd get too hot and it'd get brown, which you couldn't sell. And a couple of times as it settled down and the fat came out, there was too much for the dish and it would run into the stove. It caught fire once.

Ruby

When Col killed a pig we never had the mess other people did. I've seen him and Cliff Frost kill five pigs and dress them and hang them overnight. Then he put them on the train to send to Hobart next day. Some people always saved the blood to make black puddings. We never did. They said that when Challenors killed a pig all they lost was the squeal. When Col killed a pig, everything was provided before he started. If he wanted help, Cliff helped him mostly, but we never made any fuss about it.

You had to scald and scrape them, and the skin would be as white as snow, beautiful. We used to boil the water in an open fireplace in kerosene tins as usual. And there'd be a whole lot of posts cut up and everything ready for the fire. And I said, 'Yes, and I'd have to do six or eight tins of washing on a Monday, but there was never any posts cut up for me to boil the clothes'. But with killing a pig, everything was ready.

And when he killed a lamb – I'd see a terrible lot of fellows go and grab the shanks and they'd be dirty – but there'd never be a spot on the ones Dad did. He never got a spot on himself either.

Madge
Years before we had the butcher bus, before we left Nesdale, Dad had a car. He used to work as a stock agent and auctioneer and we went to sales with him in the car. The first we had was a 1924 Chev with a white canvas hood. He went through to Burnie to buy it. He rang Mum up and said he was coming home. But he'd never had lessons. Somebody took him out for a drive that afternoon and then he headed for home. He came back through the old Sisters Hills road and up the Grunter, that steep hill.

Ruby recalls the momentous day
He'd gone through to Burnie to a sale and it wasn't over till five o'clock. They brought the car out to the saleyard and he came back through Burnie, got his licence and rang me up. And I said, 'Don't attempt to come home'. It wasn't as if he'd gone about in cars or knew anything about them. He didn't know how to change a wheel. He had to learn all that. But he said, 'I'll get there'.

He'd had the garage built and I had the gate open. Anyway, he got into the shed and he didn't know how to stop. He thought he'd go through it! But he got the car stopped and he didn't go through his shed. He never ever had an accident.

He had three Chevs altogether. The second was the 1926 model with a black canvas hood. They were both dark blue, with a running board and celluloid windows. We had the second Chev to bring young Col home from hospital.

The butcher shop

Murray Reid (Heather's husband) with daughters Roslyn and Beryl with the Morris car

Heather
When Dad got the first car I was always a worrier and so was Mum. I always said my bladder was too close to my eyes. But we'd cover up our worries. Sometimes Dad would be driving cattle until quite late. And I used to go out to the back porch and stand looking, watching for the light to come over the hill at the school. Of course there were no other cars much in the district, so when we saw it, we'd know that was our car light and that he was on his way. And then our worries would stop. When Dad was droving cattle the dog always rode on the running board, just behind the front mudguard. Dad would drive that car for miles in low gear.

Merle
He actually did have an accident in about 1933. He was putting up for Parliament and he was setting out on his campaign, going to his first political meeting. A log had slipped off the very high bank down Trowutta Hill and he ran into it. By the time he got over the accident, his illness was showing up and they didn't know what it was. After he got really sick we sold the car. We took it down to the station at Roger River and put it on a rail truck.

Ruby
After Colin died I thought I'd buy a car. A Holden was a thousand pounds then, and I thought that if I saved £700 pounds I might be able to pay off the other three hundred. So I had this £700 nice and snug in the bank and we went to Smithton. Cliff Frost was living with me and I said, 'Cliff, I think we'll go round and buy my car'. So he said, 'All right,

Auntie Rube'. And he flew round doing things in Smithton. But it got a bit late, so he said, 'Look, Auntie Rube, I tell you what we'll do. We'll go home now and milk the cows. And we'll come back tomorrow. I won't have anything else to do then and we'll buy your car'.

Then when I got home I got an income tax bill for £390. And I was so mad! I took all the money out of the bank and paid the income tax. And I took my sister to Sydney and we had a holiday. Then I had nothing left. And afterwards I never had enough money to buy a car!

Heather
Mr Hales had the first car in the district in 1923. He had a hire car. Then Mr Malley got a car and later he took over the hire car licence. It was a big square topped sedan, a bit like a hearse. Mrs Malley drove it for a little while. But a woman driving was just not heard of. They just didn't. It was the accepted thing that the men drove and the women never thought about it. Charlie Kay at Irishtown got a car. And Pryors had a big Essex with balloon tyres. Then about four people got cars. Old Jack Ryan from the West Coast had a car fairly early and it caught fire going up the hill between Roger River and Trowutta. The burnt out frame was up on the bank there for years.

Frosts got the first one in Trowutta. It was a big grey Buick, a lovely de luxe model with beautiful woodwork, and every Sunday they would go for a drive. It was a real novelty. Cliff would always drive it. His mother and father were getting a bit old and they never learnt to drive. Cliff never liked driving and he tipped it over once. We bought it when we bought the post office. It was walk out walk in when we bought the place from old Mrs Frost. The car was only a few years old then and we sold it for fifty quid.

You bought your benzine in a four-gallon tin, like a kerosene can. There was no bowser until years later. The first was at Roger River post office. They had a bowser long before anyone else. Then there was one at Irishtown. We got one later at the post office at Trowutta.

During the war, when petrol was rationed, Mr Hales put a charcoal burner on the back of his car to save fuel. Old Mr Joiner used to burn the charcoal for him. Every now and again Mr Hales'd have to get out and stoke it up. It was a big square metal chest and it was so heavy that it cut down the mileage on the fuel consumption anyway. We used to hire him to take our badminton team to matches. It'd be your week's petrol ration to travel the 16 or 20 miles to a match. And a lot of us didn't have cars anyway.

It was the same going to dances or the pictures. There was an old school bus and everybody would crowd onto this. It was all right if you were on first and got a front seat. But the driver wouldn't go past anybody and he'd say, 'Go to the back, there's room at the back'. One night it was raining and we were going up Madison's Hill and the front wheels of the bus were coming off the ground because there was too many at the back and it had no pull. So we had to unload and the boys had to walk up.

Ruby
Hughie Maguire had a motorbike. He called at the door of the post office once and I thought I'd never seen him before and that he was the most freckled fellow I had ever seen. I said to Dad, 'Did you see all those freckles?' And he said, 'They weren't freckles. That was mud'.

Heather
Hughie Maguire was always mechanically minded and he built a three-wheeler with a box on the side out of a motorbike. They wanted to register it as a car, but he said, 'No, it's a motorbike'.

He called at the post office to pick up his girlfriend to go to a sports meeting, but she had already gone. So he said to Mum, 'Would you like a ride?' Mum was game for anything. And the whole place came to a standstill when they drove onto the sports ground.

Badminton was a wonderful thing when it came to Trowutta. That was about 1931 or 1932 and there'd been no sport that men and women could join in. There was cricket and there was football, but nothing for the women or the girls or the young people. Nothing except the country dances.

We had club shuttles and club racquets, but they were just very ordinary and I used to dream of the time I'd have my own racquet. Being a school kid, you didn't have your own money. And even afterwards, working at home you just didn't have your own money. When Uncle Cliff gave me a tiny little Jersey bull calf, I said, 'I'll rear it and sell it and I'll buy my badminton racquet'. So they used to call the calf my badminton racquet. He was a rogue, he was always getting out because he was so small and he was a worry. Dad took him and bought me this badminton racquet. It was a Spalding Speedwin and he paid two guineas for it. They all laughed when I went in to play with my racquet because they knew that it was my calf. I had this racquet all the fifty years I played badminton and I gave it to my grandson Greg in 1982.

Ruby
Every function ever held in Trowutta in the early days was at the Brydges' home in their huge room with twelve-foot ceilings. And the

sports were always on their property. The first football match in Trowutta was played on Brydges' property. They played in black and white guernseys. Two old maiden sisters there were and Tom Brydges. The other brother, Canon Brydges, who gave the land for the church, he was in Melbourne. Canon Brydges came to Australia from Ireland because of a bad chest. He got his brother Tom and sisters Mary and Lizzie to come out and they came to Trowutta.

The people of Trowutta gave them a silver teapot in appreciation of all they'd done, for making their home available. Tom was the last to die and he gave it to Dad to give to Madge, and her daughter has it now.

Heather
The name of the property was Marne Vale, a lovely sounding name. The Brydges brothers took up land here side by side. They built the house half on each property and the survey line went straight through the middle. Dad bought it after they died and used to graze cattle on it. He always had visions of writing 'Marne Vale' across on the bank of the creek in rocks painted white or in spring bulbs, so that you could read it as you approached.

But while we had it, it was burnt down. I'd seen smoke and somebody came down to tell us that the old house was on fire. Dad had been there in the morning and had burnt some rubbish in the stove. Of course nobody ever bothered to have their chimney swept. Perhaps once in all those years a chimney sweep had come through. So we reckon there must have been some rubbish in the chimney which caught alight. An insurance agent was at our house at the time and he helped Dad into his car and took him to Marne Vale, but it was too late. Nothing was saved. It was a terrific blow to Dad. He loved the place. It was one of the tragic things towards the end of his life.

When Dad first got sick, a young man who drove the service car and had all his meals at our place, brought a wireless over for him. Dad had always thought he didn't want one, but he used to listen to the wrestling, bout after bout. And I used to sit up and listen to the cricket with him.

Two old Irishmen, Danny Finnegan, the publican from the West Coast, and Tom Brydges, used to come down and play draughts with Dad. And I used to make a sponge cake with raspberry jam and sprinkle the top with icing sugar. And Tom Brydges used to say, 'Heather, I love this nice soft cake', and take piece after piece of it with his long thin fingers. I can hear him saying it now in his Irish accent. He was a man about six foot five, like a bean pole, thin as thin, and he had long thin hands and great long arms.

Dad always encouraged us to bring everybody home, the same as Mum did. And although in Mum's background Sunday was Sunday, Dad grew up in a big family where the minister used to say, 'Well, I've got to go to work now, while you have your game of cricket'. So of a Sunday night at home, when we were at the post office, there would be ten or a dozen of us around the big table in the lounge playing cards. We were encouraged to do that any night of the week. But we were never encouraged to go out and play cards. We were never allowed to gamble and if Dad saw one of those young people cheat, the whole thing was finished. That was it. No cheating. Dad was a bit like Queen Victoria. 'I am not amused.' There was a sideboard on one side of the room with a big mirror, and once Lilian was holding up her cards and Cliff could see them in the mirror. And we all laughed because he knew exactly what was coming next.

Madge
Dad's health had been cracking up but nobody knew. The doctors here hadn't seen Hodgkin's disease at that time and nobody had diagnosed it. They decided to send him to Melbourne about twelve months before he died, and I went with him. There was no way we could have got him across on the boat, he was too ill by this time. So Uncle Will took us to Western Junction and we flew over. That was my first flight in a plane and Dad's too. We went to the Royal Melbourne Hospital and that was the first time it was definitely diagnosed as Hodgkin's disease. and we knew then that there was no hope. Dad was a Justice of the Peace. After he died the people of Trowutta asked Mum if she would be a JP. She was made a JP in 1947, probably the first woman JP in Circular Head.

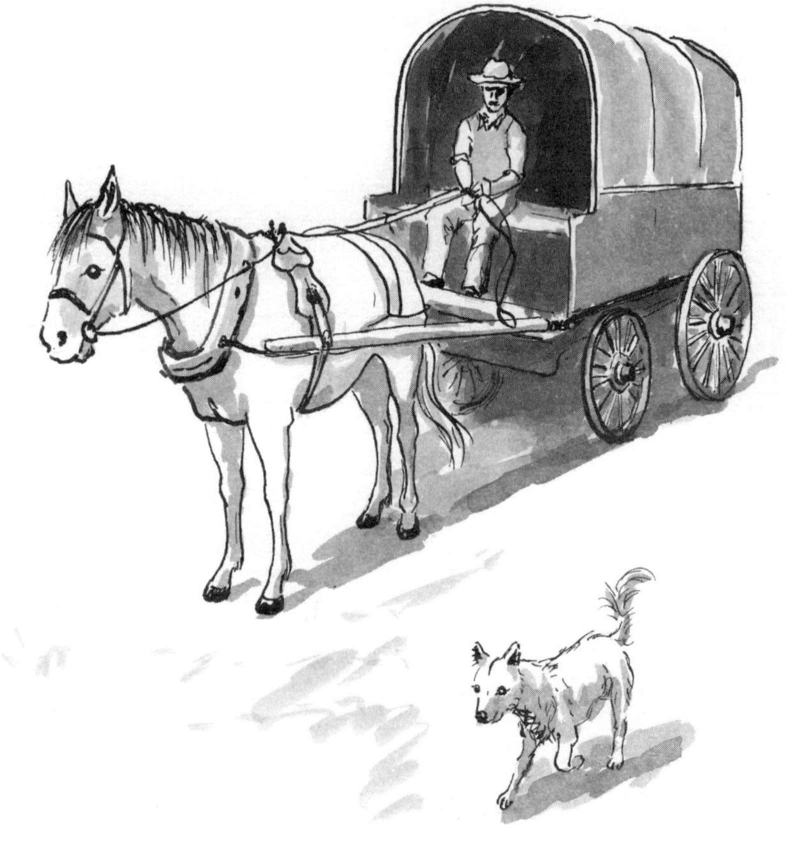

Chapter 19

Visitors

"There was always beds somewhere."

Heather

We kept a very open house. Visitors were always welcome. It didn't matter if we'd just had afternoon tea, they would say, 'Is the kettle boiling?' Sometimes I've made tea three times in the afternoon. In those days there were a lot of travellers but no eating houses, no cafes or tea rooms. They just ate at the farm houses. And in town they'd go to the post office because it was the centre.

In the early days there were a couple of Indian hawkers, Sam Ali and Joe Hassad. Joe used to stay at our place. One or two nights would be the most they'd stay. Sam and Joe had their little caravan. It looked very much like pictures of American covered wagons. Just one horse and a dog which slept under the caravan. We were always told we weren't to play with the dog. It guarded the van and Joe didn't want it to get friendly with anybody. They carried the dog a lot of the time in a sling underneath. They carried a bag of oats or chaff in this sling for their horse, and they used to sleep in the caravan.

They'd walk from the caravan to places, but they still had other things in the caravan – what you'd expect Indian hawkers to have in the early days.

They had a metal chest about three feet long and three feet high with a big canvas strap. They put the strap over their shoulder and they always walked with a sort of jog. Old Mr Hassad told me it was this little jog trot that enabled them to carry this heavy chest with ease. When they opened it up they'd lift out layer after layer of things. Thimbles, pins, knitting needles and crochet needles, braid, little plaits of darning wool and little reels of cotton and silk. Real silk too. All sorts of little things, gadgets and trinkets, on little trays with partitions. Buttons, all sorts of lovely buttons. Men used to wear fancy buttons on a fancy waistcoat in those days. Even now you'd be fascinated by them if you could see them.

In the country right out there, you'd only get to shop once in six or even twelve months. There'd perhaps be the little grocery shop. But you'd never get to see the kind of things the hawkers brought around. And it was just lovely. The kids used to crowd around. We'd kneel at this box and we'd drool over all these little things.

Ruby
In later years, about 1928, 1929, Ambrose's used to come round. That wasn't a horse, that was a motor. Ambrose's had a big van, with three men. They came once, then the big flood of 1929 washed all the bridges away. Then Arthur Ambrose came round on a bike and took orders before they got the bridges over the Black River. And from then on they always came. They used to be at our place three nights a month. It was an enormous van and they had a place for a bed in the roof where one man slept.

It was a wonderful service to the country people. Work trousers, work boots, and really good things, dress materials, pillow cases, linen, all in suitcases with straps and labelled.

Mrs Ambrose hired the Trowutta hall for a display and she stayed at our place. We slept together in the double bed – that was all we had – and she told me her whole history. They came out from Scotland. Mr Ambrose was a draper. In the Second World War the army took their van. Hector Harper who drove the mail van drove it out. Ambrose's started at Wilmot where Mrs Ambrose ran a boarding house. Eventually they got a chain of stores – at Wynyard, Burnie, Devonport, and Smithton. It's a funny thing that Ambrose's are on the coast now and started in Wilmot. And so did Coles, GJ Coles. Their first shop was at Wilmot.

Madge
And the building's still there. That was in the era when Moina was mined. They started as a little shop serving the mining community, and the people going through to the mining area.

Ruby
We used to get catalogues from David Jones', Grace Brothers and Farmers' in Sydney and one from a firm called Wake's. We always got Wynn's catalogue from Sydney too. They put out a spring/summer one and one for autumn/winter. When they came Colin would look and say, 'That's the thin end of the wedge'. We used to get his flannels from a place in Melbourne. Navy blue flannel shirts, called fireman's flannels. He was a big man, and they were a big make and they'd never shrink one bit. There was a lovely big book from Chandlers for hardware and that book would do you for years without the price going up.

Heather
After we went to the post office we never knew who would be in for meals. You never knew how many you would have. They'd come in and ask for meals at any time, sometimes quite late in the afternoon. And they were never refused. The men would have been travelling and they'd come in at half past two or three, and you always got them something, whatever it was. It didn't matter if we'd had our dinner. It didn't matter what you were doing. You knocked off and got a meal if somebody wanted it. You'd never see them go hungry. And all they paid for a three course meal was a shilling, or later eighteen pence.

We had the butcher's shop and always plenty of eggs. If we had to get a meal on the spur of the moment, we always had potatoes. So we'd have mashed potatoes and onions cut up with vinegar. We always had a bag of onions and if you didn't have much in the way of vegetables, onions were a great standby. We always had plenty of pickles and sauce and bread. So if you had cold meat and pickles and potatoes, you had a meal. And plenty of swedes. We always had swedes, really beautiful swedes.

Ruby
The bank manager used to come out from Smithton once a month, and eventually once a week. He used to come to our place and we'd give him the front room, so people who wanted to interview him could come and see him. I used to let Mr Gillies have the office and I locked him in one day. I just walked past and saw the office door ajar.

We always kept it locked so I pulled it shut and turned the key before he could sing out. It was quite a while before he could make us hear! Sometimes he used to bring his wife. The day the bank manager was coming there was always afternoon tea in the front room for him and his wife.

Heather

At Lileah the bank manager used to come out once a week and collect the money. He had a pistol he used to carry and a little portmanteau for carrying the money. But he'd always fold it and put it in his pocket. 'And now,' he said, 'If I'm held up they can have the bag'. He had all the money 'on his pusson'.

The dentist, Mr Lucadou Wells, came once a month to Trowutta from Burnie. He used our sitting room. He'd be there for a couple of hours and whoever wanted dental attention 'd come to our sitting room. And there was a chair, just a very ordinary armchair – it was almost history, that chair – where he'd extract teeth. We always kept the kettle boiling for him in the kitchen and he'd come out and get hot water. He used to do impressions for dentures, extractions, the lot. And you'd hear the plop, plop, plop as the teeth dropped into the basin. He always threw them out into the garden afterwards, then he'd come into the kitchen and wash the basin. He'd have his dinner with us and when he left there'd be five shillings on the table.

There was an old drover, Mr Ferguson, used to stay with us. He had a long white beard. There'd be a drive of cattle going next morning, so he'd ride his horse out from Smithton, stay the night, then before daylight he'd be up for a cooked breakfast before he got the cattle on the road to drive them to a sale somewhere. He used to show us kids how to crack a whip and he used to plait whips. He made one for our brother Col. It had a polished blackwood handle and he'd put CP on the handle in pins with the heads just showing. Col always went off carrying that whip to the sales with Dad.

Another that used to stay with us was the old surveyor, Mr K.M. Harrison. He surveyed most of Circular Head, all Trowutta and way back in the bush beyond. He had a lot to do with the naming of places and he told me their Aboriginal meanings. Trowutta means flint; Nabageena means sunny hills and so does Lileah. Marrawah means one. He showed me the theodolite and how it worked and what he did with it. And he showed me how he measured. That was the first time I'd heard the word theodolite and I thought, 'What a lovely word'. I was always great cobbers with these chaps. They'd come regularly and I used to talk to them and learned a lot from them.

Ruby

In the real early days we had lots of travellers. We always felt they were a necessary evil, because they had all the time in the world, and often wouldn't come out to our place until after the shops closed at night. Ours was one they could do because they knew we'd be there. We had to be until eight o'clock. The tea travellers would mostly walk. They'd stay a night or perhaps two. Some people wouldn't have room for them but they were always welcome at our place. Atcheley and Dawson were the two travellers for Griffiths tea. One came in a cart and horse, like a jinker, and gave the kids a ride home from school. Another tea traveller was Mr Ponsonby. I went to school with his father in Zeehan. I remember we had some Robur tea and somebody spilt some on the table cloth. And he said, 'Now see Robur stain'. It was evidently full of tannin and it stained.

We had the Cadbury traveller. We had Genders, the hardware firm. And we had Johnson and Wilmot. They were wholesale groceries and liquor. But we didn't handle liquor. The merchants from Stanley, Jack Holmes and Jack Horne, used to come round, to take orders for the crops. Sometimes there'd be a representative from Massey Harris or Sunshine Harvesters, or one of those big farming machinery firms, trying to sell new equipment.

One day I remember – it was somebody's birthday – and I made a lemon cake in a great big dish. I put it on the window sill to cool and the dog came and ate it. So I threw the rest of it to the dog and had to bake another one. I had visitors that morning too!

The worst thing that ever happened was that a knock came at the door when I had a dish of fat from the butcher shop I'd been melting down

surveyor using a theodolite

in the oven, and I'd stood it on a biscuit tin on the table. And these four men came in wanting dinner. It was getting late so I hurried to get it ready and knocked the dish of fat. And it spilled all over the table, all over the floor, up the wall, even on the window! So I tipped a bucket of cold water over it, then scraped it up on the shovel. Then I had to get the dinner ready.

Mostly I didn't charge them, but they usually left two shillings on the table. I never used to charge Mr Smith. He often used to stay the night and he'd pay something. He said, 'Don't you be silly. Before they leave the office, they go and put the two shillings in their pocket for their meal allowance and you might as well have it as them'. Heather once charged someone two and sixpence and he never came again!

When there was a parliamentary campaign they used to make our place in Trowutta their headquarters. They'd advertise that they'd be there and I'd give them the front room for their interviews. They'd have their tea at our place and come back after the meeting in the hall. The voting used to be in the hall at Trowutta. They liked to get returned soldiers to be polling clerks.

Heather
At Lileah, Murray and his brother were always the poll clerks. We had the voting at the school, then we found it was better and easier to do it at home. They used to pay us for the room and for doing it. Murray could help me in between then, because an election brought everybody out and it was a terribly busy day.

At Trowutta we never had the house to ourselves. Never. We always had somebody and we'd be cooking for crowds and crowds. Sometimes there was two beds in the lounge and there was beds in the passage and there was a double bed and sometimes two single beds in my room, the big back bedroom. Sometimes when we had visitors, Mum'd tack some blankets up along the front verandah and put beds behind that. There was always beds somewhere. The girls would always come home for their school holidays and often they'd bring others. When they were training as teachers, their friends were teachers.

Of course there were schools in every little district and there'd be a phone call and Madge'd say, 'So-and-so's been transferred to Nabageena, somebody's been transferred to Forest, somebody's been transferred to Smithton'. So we'd get in touch with them and give them a meal. And they'd be pretty lonely, so back they'd come for the weekend. Sometimes there'd be about five or six girls for the weekend.

We always had a big fire towards evening up in the top room and when Dad was sick, one night Mum went to get this big log. It was about three feet long and had a great spike on one end. But it wasn't half as heavy as it looked, because it was hollow. She got as far as the back door and somebody in a raincape was leaning with his arms on the architrave each side. Mum just thought it was Hector Harper who drove the mail bus and came to us for meals. So she walked up and gave him a prod with the end of this big black log. And he jumped round, threw up his arms and the words never came out, seeing this woman with this great log! And it was the young curate! Poor old Dad looked real confused. But Mum was laughing so much she couldn't even walk up the passage straight.

Ruby concluded the story
There was a big box in the passage and I sat down killing myself laughing. Hughie Maguire was there, courting the schoolteacher who boarded with us, and he thought I'd got that far and couldn't carry it. So he came and took the log and said, 'Why didn't you send me for the wood?' 'But it was as light as a feather. Some of the things that happened, really and truly Steele Rudd had nothing on me!

After Dad died I had all these teenagers and everybody had to bring their friends home, because I wouldn't let them go off. I just made rules for the house, and they'd sit by the fire at night and eat apples, and go into the shop and buy six penn'orth of lollies. They'd eat lollies and apples. And play cards.

Heather
During the war my cousin joined up and his wife went back to work in Melbourne, and they sent their little boy to live with us for two or three years. Mum really reared him. We had Auntie Pearl's daughter too. They were living in Melbourne working for the war effort and Pearl was worried about having children there. Then Mum reared a baby whose mother died when he was a few hours old. Kevin came to us straight out of hospital, barely three weeks old. We reared him until he was nine months. I looked after him in the daytime and Mum looked after him at night. He cried and cried, he had a terrible lot of trouble with his bottle. But we used to get a bit of comfort looking after him, when Dad was so sick.

My cousin Cliff Frost lived with us during that time. Cliff'd had an apprenticeship as a blacksmith in Melbourne, but he hated it and came back after a few months. About the same time the Frosts left their farm and went to live in Melbourne, so he lived with us and worked on our farm. Nine years he was with us.

Ruby

Before we went to the post office we had the two Rainbow girls, Win and Jean, with us for six months. Their father was a clerk at a mill, and when it closed they shifted to Stanley. They had seven children and the little house in Stanley only held the rest of them. Win was the oldest and she had an old head on young shoulders. She was very, very responsible. Her mother had a lot of babies and she had to bear the brunt of it. I remember having six little girls to get ready to go to a picnic, iron their dresses and everything. But they were good kiddies. My word they could work and I missed them when they left.

There was one lady when we were at the post office and she'd got pretty sick. She couldn't stand but she could walk and she'd walk down to my place, about a mile and a half. She had a little stool she carried. And I said, 'Now don't go carrying that seat with you. Just come inside and sit down in the kitchen and I'll make you a cuppa'. She was a dear. She used to come every Saturday about eleven o'clock to wait for the mail which came at 1.30. I always had a bowl of soup for her and nearly always I gave her dinner. But there was a spiteful old woman who bought Gran Pacey's place. She used to be sitting on her verandah and one day she said to this dear old woman, 'Do you go down to Mrs Pauls's to get your dinner?' After that she never came again.

This old woman who bought mother's house was frightened to go to the toilet there. It wasn't a tippy tin, it was the old cesspit. She could have put in a septic, but she was too mean and stuck to her money. Instead she used to come over to my place several times a day and use my toilet! And she'd say, 'I'll have to do something about my toilet'. I didn't mean to offend her, but I said, 'Well, you'd better do something, with winter coming'. So then she bought a couple of plastic buckets!

Chapter 20

Weddings and christenings

"Everybody's egg beaters were going non-stop for weeks."

Ruby

There was no refrigeration when Madge and Heather and Merle got married. Lilian was married in Launceston so there was no big fuss for her. But everybody's egg beaters were going, especially when Heather got married. Going non-stop for a couple of weeks.

When Merle was getting married, she didn't want just an ordinary reception, she wanted a ball. She said, 'Don't ask just the people. Ask all the children as well'. She was a teacher, so we got 400 cards to send out. And I made forty dozen sausage rolls. We got a nice glass rolling pin and lovely sausage rolls we made with that. Mother used to use a bottle. Anyway, there weren't any sausage rolls left over!

Everybody helped us. Peg, Merle's sister-in-law to be, cooked for three days at our place. Marge Howard made lots of little butterfly cakes. She scooped the top of them and put raspberry jam and cream and put the top back on and iced them with a little lemon icing. They were beautiful. We set the table right down the middle of the hall. And we got an orchestra with quite a few players. They came from Marrawah.

Heather
Madge and I were both married in the church at Irishtown. It was a beautiful church. My husband Murray was the first baby baptised there. We had our wedding breakfast at home and we had to overflow into two rooms. We had seventy guests. We took all the furniture out so there was nothing in them but the tables. Afterwards we had a big dance at night in the hall, an open night. We didn't send invitations for that. The lady who played the piano was Mrs Moore.

Ruby describes the preparations for supper
Five loaves of bread were supposed to come out on the bus for the wedding dance supper. We had a big ham we'd cooked for the wedding. And we had the wedding breakfast off it and were going to cut sandwiches for the supper. Then this bread didn't come and we had the ham going begging. But it didn't beg for long! I took big tins of biscuits and jars of coloured onions out of the shop, and pickles, and we had to make do with that. Mary Morice, who helped in the post office, used to help with everything, and she brought little cakes. So we had little cakes and big cakes and things that other people made. But we still ran out of food and had to cut up the top tier of the wedding cake to make enough for supper.

Heather
We had the reception for Madge's wedding at home too, but we didn't have anything in the hall afterwards. You see, Madge had been away. But Merle and I were part of Trowutta all our life. Merle had been away to high school, but at Smithton, and she was always more or less at home at weekends. So after Madge's wedding we collected up all the young people and everybody we could and two or three carloads went into Smithton to a dance in the Church of England hall. Then we landed home to Pauls' for supper afterwards. We nearly always landed home to our place after things. Mum was in bed, but that didn't matter.

Ruby
Madge had a wonderful kitchen tea. And we didn't expect that because she'd been away since she was just about to turn twelve. But she

always came home for holidays and went to anything that was on. So Wilfred Crole said, 'We'll have a kitchen tea for Madge'. Kitchen teas were a tradition for the whole district to join in. That was always a big dance. Everybody came. Really good gifts people brought. If they weren't coming to the wedding, a lot of them made them wedding presents. But mainly things for the kitchen, always a kitchen tea, never a pantry tea or bathroom tea, like you have now. Anything from a tea strainer to cutlery and crockery. Beautiful table cloths and things you got. Merle got three sets of saucepans. Silver was just coming back in and I don't know how many silver sugar basins she got. And a silver tray. Heather was married in wartime and things were a bit hard to get then, but we had a very nice evening. Mrs Moore played for Heather's kitchen tea too.

Then after the bride and groom got back from their honeymoon there was always another do and that was a tin-kettling. It usually started in the house and finished up in the hall. We'd go with tins and cans and we'd bang, always trying to surprise them, but generally they knew. They'd look surprised, yes, but they always knew it would come sometime.

The night they tin-kettled Murray and Heather at Lileah, they expected them, and they finished up over in the school.

I told you I was married in a hurry and afterwards I was still at home and Col used to work in Irishtown during the week and come out to Trowutta every weekend. And every Saturday night for three weeks after we were married we expected them to come out, but it was terrible storms and rain and hail. When they did come we'd just got into bed. They came at half past twelve and it was so wet and so bad that they had to stay all night. And they sang and went on until I was ready to drop. But they all thought I wanted to go to bed because I was just married!

It was very difficult to get clothes for Heather's wartime wedding, because of the rationing. You had to have coupons for the material, so many coupons per yard, and she had two bridesmaids. So Gran Pacey gave enough coupons for the material for the wedding frock, and some towards the girls. 'I'll not be wanting anything', Gran Pacey said. She was saving her coupons to give Heather enough and that's how they were able to have long frocks. A lady at Nabageena, a widow with four grown-up children, gave Murray petrol coupons for the extra running about he was doing for the wedding, because she didn't need them.

When Lilian got married, Hugh was in the air force. He'd gone away and when he came back, they decided to be married. So Lilian rang me on this Sunday and said, 'I'm being married on Wednesday'.

Lilian

We rang Mum to tell her we were engaged and had the ring. But we were doing the right thing and Hugh wanted to ask Mum could he marry her daughter. Where I was boarding in Launceston the phone was in the hall and everyone was going up and down and at Trowutta there was a storm and the rain on the roof was so loud Mum could hardly hear. And there was poor Hugh trying to make Mum understand he was asking for her daughter's hand!

It was near the end of the war and clothes were very scarce with rationing and there were only a couple of wedding dresses in Launceston. But it was my luck that one of them just fitted me – cream satin, the full thing.

Ruby

I didn't have a thing to wear and I had to arrange about getting to Launceston for the wedding and my hair was awful. So I said to my sister Syl, 'You've got a rinse that you put through your hair, haven't you?' She looked a bit funny, but she said, 'Oh, yes'. And she brought over this packet of stuff and I washed my hair in it. And I came out as red as a bit of turkey twill!

Well, I scrubbed and I used sandsoap and nothing would take it out. Fortunately it was when we were wearing tam-o'-shanters, and I had this black felt tam-o'-shanter. So I covered my head with that. And I sent in to Arthur Ambrose's store in Smithton and said, 'Send me out some dresses and a pair of shoes'. They sent out three frocks and there was only one that would go on me, and that was tight. So Arthur Ambrose said, 'I'll run a few suits out to Irishtown and you can try them on in the waiting room. There's half an hour between the bus and the train'. Anyway he didn't get there for some reason. Perhaps when he looked he didn't have anything to fit me, but they never let me know. Fortunately I'd taken the one dress with me and a fur coat.

And the shoes were too tight, but I'll tell you what I did. I put them in a big dish of soapy water – you don't do that to shoes. But I soaked them and soaked them and I put them on and walked about until they were dry. But they were hurting me all the way through in the train! I went the morning of the wedding – she was being married at seven. Pearl and Syl came with me. Heather and Merle went the day before. Merle had to apply for leave but she didn't have time to wait for it, so she just had to close her school.

Heather
Merle was bridesmaid, but Lilian had the forethought to tell me to bring my wedding frock in case she couldn't get a dress. Well, we walked Launceston and realised we couldn't do anything about a new one, so we set to that night to make my wedding frock look like a bridesmaid's. Anyhow, it did the job. Lilian had bought herself her wedding gown and the assistant had said it was very exclusive and she wouldn't see another one like it. But next day when we were looking for the bridesmaid's frock, we found two exactly the same. Anyway, everyone Lilian knew wanted to borrow it afterwards.

Heather recalls problems with wedding cakes
When Madge was married we had difficulties with the icing on the wedding cake. The morning of the wedding, after I'd assembled the cake, we had the table set and everything ready for the wedding breakfast, and when we went in, the cake had started to topple. It was a three decker and the icing wouldn't hold the weight of the top deck. I had the same problem with Cliff Frost's wedding cake. It was during the war and you couldn't buy the icing and roll it out like you do now. It was half cornflour and it wouldn't hold its shape. You just couldn't force it through the forcer. My hand was all blistered trying. Then the legs started to slip and I'd have to straighten it up again. It was a real shame because it was a beautiful cake. Somebody else had the same problem, so I know it wasn't just me.

Ruby
Gran Porteus and I made my wedding cake. It was three tiers and Syl iced it. Grandma stoned the raisins and we cooked it in the old camp oven. It was a nice cake, but you couldn't buy pillars or anything like that. So Grandfather cut up an old towel rail to make the pillars and he didn't get them real flush. Gran iced them and put them on the cake, but it kept going a bit to one side. We made do somehow. Probably the girls used them later on for some cake. It was a shame to cut up the towel rail. They were lovely things those towel rails. I wish I had it now. George Porteus made some pillars once out of a broomstick and Heather iced them. She iced some cotton reels another time. You had to make do with whatever you could get.

Everybody that was at the church for a christening always came home afterwards. They'd have a special afternoon, and friends in, but they wouldn't make a great thing about it. When we had church in the hall, the christenings were there. And for years they used a white crockery basin. It was always called the christening bowl and it came from Gran's. It was real bone china. There was gold round the rim and another narrow gold band around the inside, and a gold shamrock in the middle at the bottom.

The children all had a special outfit for their christening. I remember making a cream radienta dress for one. Radienta was a very fine woollen material and it never shrank. There was a cream voile that used to shrink, and a woollen one too. But this radienta never shrank. It was very expensive, so I used to line the sleeves and the yoke, so the dress wouldn't wear out in a hurry. It was very nicely made with three rows of pin tucks across the bottom above the hem. And one had a silk dress that Col's sister sent. And they all wore the Granny Paul bonnet. Colin had cream rompers when he was christened. I embroidered them with a row of circles entwined and I drew the three circles with an egg cup. Then I smocked them across the front.

People always came back to the house for a cup of tea after a funeral too, if they'd travelled a distance. They still do.

Chapter 21

Remedies and recipes

"There was always a blue bottle of castor oil."

Heather

There was always a blue bottle of castor oil, a bottle of olive oil, a bottle of eucalyptus, some licorice powder, and a tin of Rexona. Rexona was an ointment in a triangular tin with just slightly rounded corners. Then there was Zambuk, another ointment. That was your medicine chest. And Epsom salts of course, and iodine. Iodine got poured into everything, all your cuts, everything. My word, it used to sting.

Ruby

It won't sting if you put it in while the cut's still warm. I remember Minnie Sawley falling and skinning all her knees on the gravel and we put a bandage on and poured iodine all over. It was all right for about an hour, then it started to hurt and she had to take it off.

Carbolic oil, we always had. And boracic acid, and sulphur. Sulphur was a yellow powder. It was really good for sore throats. For a gargle we used to put a little bit of sulphur, a little bit of soda, a little bit of salt and the same quantity of oil, all in warm water and gargle.

I remember Mother used to get very bad throats. They were very painful. She would make a cornet from a small square of paper, put the sulphur in it and someone would blow through the wide end down her throat through the point. They were so frightened of diphtheria, that's when they used sulphur.

When the kids had a cold, I used to put three drops of eucalyptus on sugar. Heather dosed herself one night, probably more than three drops, and nearly choked, breathing in as she went to take it. When they had whooping cough I used to put sugar on a spoon then fill the spoon with olive oil and three drops of eucalyptus. I don't think it did much good really. Minnie Sawley was one of the worst cases of whooping cough I've ever seen. As soon as she'd get up from the table she'd have to run and be sick everywhere. Her mother took her to Dr Franklin in Smithton and told him how bad she was and he said, 'Take her home, put a coat on her, cover her hands, cover her legs right up with long stockings, put a bonnet on her and cover her ears, just leave her face out and let her go out to play. Let her go out all the time.' And you know, she got better pretty fast, she did really. She'd skip about outside, it didn't matter what the weather was like, so long as she didn't get wet.

In the olden days at Zeehan scarlet fever was a dreadful thing. Scarlatina was a mild form something the same. But when it was scarlet fever it was bad. There was scarlet fever and measles and whooping cough in Trowutta, but I never remember diphtheria, though there was a case in Irishtown. And mumps. Heather was nearly grown up when we had mumps. Cliff Frost was staying at my place when he got them and he kicked his bed to pieces. So I took him out of that bed, led him by the arm and brought him into another bed, and he was there for a week before he knew me. He was in bed in one room and Heather was in bed in another. And I was running the post office and the store and all the rest as usual.

There were several cases of pneumonia. Dad had pneumonia once and I didn't realise how sick he was. And that was when a doctor told us to use creosote. You had to have so many drops in milk. It was an awful smell. Em's husband had miner's phthisis and it cured him. Dad took that creosote for a long time. And it did him a lot of good. Cathy Ryan fell off a gate post and got what they called hip disease, which was TB of the hip. She was on a bed with wheels and they took her everywhere on it for easily twelve months. Absolute rest. She got better although it left her with a limp. That's what Hoppy Nichols had too.

Cliff Frost got croup, we all got croup. One of the reasons we got bad colds and croup was that there was so much water about then and it would soak right through our boots. I can remember going to school in Zeehan with a terrible croupy cough and the teachers never took any notice. We used to have a bottle of medicine called Granny Chamberlain's. You'd keep giving it to the person, a spoonful at a time until they were sick and that would bring up all the phlegm.

Heather
I remember Madge waking up with croup. There was no fire and no electricity and Mum warmed a tablespoon over the lamp and put olive oil and sugar and eucalyptus on the warm spoon.

Another thing we had in our medicine chest was linseed meal for poultices. It was used for splinters or inflammation or boils, anything that wanted drawing out. And castor oil. I remember how castor oil would repeat. I could never keep it down. One thing we used to get was called liniment eucalyptus. It was red and used mostly for rubs. It would really burn. And we used to have bluestone. If you got a piece of proud flesh in a sore it would burn it off. Our medicine chest was important in the house. You couldn't just run out to a chemist. There was just nothing else available. Those old home remedies are coming back again now. People are realising the value of them.

Ruby
When Colin was away the year his mother was dying and left me with our four little girls, I was spring-cleaning before he came home. I had a little shelf right up near the roof of the kitchen where I put all the medicines and I had to climb on the table to get them. Well, I put them down on the table to clean this shelf. And Lilian was very fond of these three drops of eucalyptus on sugar I gave them for colds. And she got the bottle of eucalyptus and tipped it up. I don't know how much she drank. The bottle was half empty but she had it all down the front of her. I thought I'd see what happened and I let her go. She had Ralph Butler with her and they went outside to play. Soon he brought her in by the hand and said, 'There's something the matter with Lilian'. Her eyes were rolling. Her head would go one way and her eyes would go the other.

We didn't have the phone. Somebody went for Gran and Mrs Frost. I remember them coming up in the jinker with their hair flying and their hats falling off, and people running from everywhere. I knew I had to make her sick. She had my fingers nearly bitten off, poor little Lilian. When Auntie Phyllis came she said, 'Break two eggs and take the whites, and pour that down her throat'.

And I did. And she brought up all the eucalyptus stuck to the whites of the eggs. And I'm sure that saved her life.

They had to go right down to the post office, two miles away, to ring the doctor and he just told us to make her sick. Mustard and water, warm soapy water. I don't know what – all we gave her, the poor little kid. 'Don't let her go to sleep. Walk her about', he said. 'There's nothing more I can do, but I'll come out if you want me.'

But all the eucalyptus came up stuck to the egg white. It was the only thing that brought it up. So we didn't bother getting him out. After a few hours she was so exhausted, but I was frightened to let her go to sleep till nine o'clock at night. Eventually, Phyllis, my oldest sister, said, 'She's too exhausted, she's got to go to sleep'.

When her father came home about two days afterwards he took one look and said, 'What's the matter with Lilian?' And I said, 'Well, you nearly didn't have her'. I knew I'd get the blame. I'd only turned my back a minute. But Lilian said, 'We won't talk about that any more'.

I remember Gran's boots that day. She hadn't stopped to find her buttonhook and she'd buttoned them up with a hairpin instead. If you lost the buttonhook, you used a hairpin. And the hairpin was still out of her head. It was still around the button!

When I used to bake my bread, I never put anything but flour and salt in it, and potato. For baking there was no compressed or dried yeast and we always made our own. You'd never use the last little bit in your yeast bottle, that was your starting yeast. You'd save the water off the potatoes you boiled and you'd mash a good half or even a whole potato in with it very fine. Sometimes you'd put it through a strainer and that's what you'd mix with the bread. We used to get much better flour in those days. I don't know whether it wasn't so refined, but it was much nicer.

When you had the bread dough and you'd have plenty, I'd save a great big pie dish to cook Johnny cakes for breakfast. Cliff still talks about it. You'd take a piece and roll it out fairly thin and drop it into real hot fat. And it would come up as brown as anything. You'd turn it over once and if you had a good pan of boiling fat they'd cook in just a few minutes. They wouldn't be a bit heavy, they'd be light, and we all loved them.

We put slabs of butter on them while they were still hot and the butter would be just dripping out of them. They looked like a fried scone. Some people called them muffins.

Sometimes if we were short of bread on a Friday, we'd make an ordinary scone. You didn't have as much fat for them. They didn't have the flavour of the ones made with bread dough. Sometimes that's what we'd have for tea on a Saturday night. After tea we'd bake the bread dough and have lovely fresh crusty bread on Sunday. We nearly always baked twice a week. You baked when you had a loaf left and you thought you'd have to replenish.

Irish soda bread I used to make in the camp oven, two ounces of soda to four or five cups of flour, the dough just patted together three to four inches thick. The flour was supposed to be sifted seven times, but I only did it three or four times. I used to keep it ready in a great big crock. It was very handy. Irish tea bread was mixed with cold tea. Barm brack it was called. It was a sort of sweet fruit loaf. You soak the fruit in cold tea overnight and then just mix in the flour and honey and an egg.

Boxtie was another Irish dish and the real Irish potato cakes. Boxtie is made of potato, mashed and grated. You boil so much potato and mash it like potato cake. Then you grate the same quantity of potato and put it in a thin cloth and wring all the moisture out. You mix the two and put in so much flour and a bit of salt and work it up and make it into cakes and boil it. It's like India rubber. It's most delightful stuff.

We made them about three inches across and about three quarters of an inch thick. You'd boil them for about twenty minutes, then you took them out and browned them or toasted them in front of the fire. We always had an open fire and a big toasting fork. But mostly they browned them on the pan or in the camp oven. In Ireland they used to send them out to the men in the paddock. They'd put these mats on the donkey's back and put the boxtie under to keep hot till it got out to the men. And there was a saying in our family, 'Slaws of boxtie between the mats and the ass'. That meant there was plenty of something.

Another great favourite was our potato cake, the Irish potato cake. My mother used to make that when the kids were only very tiny, and everybody that ever belonged to us got used to potato cake and we still make it. It takes a bit of effort. You work it like you would bread, knead it together. You can roll it with a rolling pin but it doesn't seem right, somehow. But you've got to keep it from breaking round the edges and my mother used to do it with the back of her hand. You'd flatten it to about half an inch thick and you'd cook it slowly in the camp oven. There's no way you can make it on the pan that's anything like as good.

You greased the oven, not a lot. You don't swim it in fat. Dripping, you wouldn't waste butter on it. And when it's cooked you'd never think of just buttering it. You cut a round hole in the middle nearly right through and you put a great big piece of butter in it. Then you take out a wedge, a farrel we call it, and each piece you take on your fork you roll in the butter. That's the real Irish way. It was very very popular but perhaps it was because we were brought up to it.

The recipe is just plain boiled potatoes with a little bit of salt in them, drained very dry and mashed very finely. You don't want any lumps. No milk, no butter. Then you work in enough plain flour, about the same amount of flour as potato, with your hands to make a paste that you can roll out. You couldn't work it in with anything else. Then you cook it in a hot greased pan fairly slowly and by the time it's done you hope somebody will have the table set and then you serve it very hot with lashes of butter. It makes a complete meal. You never want anything more.

We also made potato puffs with potatoes that were mashed with milk whipped into them.

Potato pastry is a very nice thing if you have a little bit of cold meat to use up. You work a cup of self-raising flour and a little bit of milk or water, whatever you've got, and roll it out fairly thin. You wouldn't have it too thick and you cut it out with a saucepan lid, not a very big saucepan. You mince all your cold meat, drop it on the pastry and turn it over like a pasty. You roll that with a rolling pin and make it fairly flat and fry that. That was one of the things we used to do to use up the cold meat because you had to make an extra meal out of the cold roast and it would make quite a good substantial meal. It was nearly always to use up the roast beef. Some people just used to make a stew out of it. That was John Paul's 'dead meat stew'. The meat was cooked twice.

boiler

Pearl used to make a potato pie – shepherd's pie. She always had to make one for Lilian when she came home. The kids used to have what they called a beano. Pearl had a great big open fireplace in the wash house and they used to roast potatoes and onions in the fire. She'd make a potato pie for their tea before they went out to have their beano for supper.

I made a lot of soup because we had the butcher's shop. I used to boil the bones in a boiler two feet six long. It was at Frosts' and it had a little hole in the side. We used to stick a match in it. It was a fault in the casting. But there'd be these huge pots of bones, big marrow bones and rib bones and everything. People used to boil a marrow bone. It would be open at one end and you made a little paste and put it over the top, and you boiled the bone, took the marrow out and spread it on toast, with salt and pepper.

On Saturdays we always made cake, a light fruit cake. Saturday cake we used to call it. I creamed the butter and sugar with my hands. There were no whirly egg beaters in the early days, no wooden spoons unless you made one. So that's what we did. We'd cream the butter and sugar with our hands, then beat the eggs into it and add the flour and milk. I used four eggs and a cup of milk. And cooked it in a big meat dish.

What I make now is four ounces of butter, two eggs and one cup of self-raising flour. But you used to use plain flour with cream of tartar. Two teaspoons of cream of tartar to one of soda to a full sifter of flour. Cream of tartar was lighter and smooth. Soda was sort of heavier and quite often lumpy. You'd always put the soda in your hand and grind it with the back of a spoon.

Heather
Our cream biscuits we'd start to make perhaps before we washed up the breakfast dishes. We used to put a cup of cream and a cup of sugar in the mixing bowl, and each time you went past through the day you'd give it a stir. And by the time you were ready to cook it in the afternoon the sugar was all dissolved nicely and it was like a very thick creamy syrup. Then you just stirred in enough plain flour with a little bit of cream of tartar and soda.

A lot of the time we didn't use vanilla, because Dad didn't like vanilla. He liked just the plain flavour of the cream and sugar and flour. They were crisper than a shortbread, but a good plain biscuit. Sometimes we'd ice them, sometimes we'd put them together with jam. They were the first thing we learnt to make. We were allowed to roll them out and cut them with our own biscuit cutters. Mine was a rabbit, Madge's was a horse, Lilian's was the chicken and Merle's was the dog. We all had our own. Auntie Phyllis brought them from Melbourne for us. Mine was the best because there was no waste of dough. We used that the most because it saved rolling out so many times.

Ruby Paul c. 1960

Chapter 22

Royals and a medal

"He should have milked his cows first."

Heather

When the Duke of Gloucester visited in 1934 he only came as far as Burnie. The government had prepared a royal train for the tour, and they ran a train from Trowutta to Burnie. It had to go into Stanley and out again and then right through to Burnie. We had to catch it at some unearthly hour of the morning, and the Trowutta station was down on the flat at Roger River so we had to leave home at daylight. Mum had packed a huge hamper for our lunch and it was such an excursion. It was the first time we'd ever been to Burnie!

All the schools from along the route were going. There were children everywhere. And when the Duke arrived on the Burnie recreation ground, now the West Park oval, he was in a brown pinstriped suit. I'll never forget the disappointment of all the children, because we were expecting a prince in all his regalia. We felt so let down because this was such a big day. We all had flags and ribbons and badges. 'Wave to the duke', the officials were calling. And here was this man who wasn't any different from all the others!

It must have been nine or ten o'clock at night by the time we got home, and a lot of the kids were asleep. We'd taken rugs. Somebody met us at the train. It was a full day, a day and a half really, crowded into one day. And we were just so tired and disappointed.

In comparison, when our girls were small, we took them ourselves to see the Queen. It was 1954, the first official visit of Queen Elizabeth and Prince Philip. There were crowds and crowds of people from right through the district and the Queen was to arrive at the Wynyard airport. We couldn't get a vantage point there, so we took up our position at the corner of the main street. Everybody had new outfits to wear because the Queen was coming. Our girls were dressed one in a pink and one in a blue frock with a tiny floral pattern. And we waited and waited. It seemed that the Queen was airsick and they circled Wynyard for half an hour trying to get her settled on medication before she arrived in front of all these crowds.

There were hundreds of children and hundreds of parents, and no one wanted to move in case they lost their spot. And the children got so restless. Then we saw the aircraft land and we knew it wouldn't be very long. First of all there was the motorcycle escort and then the Queen's car came, an open car. We could see her quite close and she was waving. She had a beautiful grey coat with lemon dress and yellow gloves. She looked so beautiful but so tired. I thought, 'Oh dear, she looks tired'. The poor thing, I felt so sorry for her.

We followed her to the recreation ground where all the children were able to mass in the centre of the oval, and she drove round again in the car in front of the dais. And it was such a celebration! Then she was to have afternoon tea in Burnie at a civic reception. So we followed the royal car right through and then went on and spent the rest of the day with Murray's father and mother. We had a wonderful day compared with the let-down of the Duke of Gloucester.

Ruby
I can remember the coronation of Edward VII. We all got a medal, a coronation medal. It was silver, real big and had a red, white and blue ribbon. It was in the box with all the things that got stolen at Strahan. There was a holiday. I remember Pearl was a very little girl and she had a new dress and some of us gave her our medals to wear.

When it was George the Fifth's coronation Charlie and I were coming home on the train to Zeehan for a visit. We got to Boko Siding, away out. There was nowhere else to pass on that line so we were there all day waiting for the three through trains from Burnie. A few other people were in another carriage and everybody was bored. We didn't know what to do, so we learnt to play Red Dog, a gambling game with cards. And we taught this other carriageful and played Red Dog all the day. There was a shed and a few men working on the railway but no toilets or anything. Charlie went away over on the hill behind some trees and it was pretty rough going, so we asked these men if there was a toilet nearby. 'No', they said. 'Just go behind the shed, you'll be all right'. So that was Coronation Day!

When the Queen came out with Prince Philip, there was a girl from Trowutta who made this big striped tiger. It was put up with the rest of the decorations across the street and Prince Philip was greatly taken by this thylacine. Then afterwards somebody stole it. There was a great big fuss about it. They got it back and used it when Prince Philip came again.

After I closed the shop Col had it for a while and then Grace Frost. But I still had the post office. If I wanted to go away, Madge and her husband would take over for a while. And Madge took over when I broke my hip. It was a Saturday night. I'd climbed up on a chair to wind the clock and had a fall. It was a very bad break evidently but something worse could have happened.

Heather

Mum was in hospital when she was notified that she'd got the Imperial Service Medal. Col and Shirl were going to milk when they got the telegram. And of course, being a telegram for Mum, Col thought it was bad news so he opened it. He rang for me to go through it and said, 'There's a telegram here for Mum and wait till I read you what it says'. He said, 'I've opened it, now what'll I do with it?' I said, 'You'll have to take it in to her'.

Ruby

I didn't take a bit of notice of it. He should have milked his cows first. Into the hospital they came rushing about six o'clock or half past and I said, 'Whatever's gone wrong? What's happened?' And he was waggling this telegram and all the nurses came in and I made them put it in my Bible, in case somebody else read it. One of the nurses did find it and showed it to the surgeon next morning. And he said, 'Well, congratulations'. He didn't think much of those sort of things.

Reverse of Imperial Service Medal for Faithful Service

After I came out of hospital it was quite a long time before the presentation of the medal at Government House in Hobart. They said I could have two guests, two members of the family. I had to submit their names and we got official invitations. It was very nice. They showed us over Government House and there was a band all in red coats. The Governor told us all that he'd done since he came there and he was congratulating me.

'Well, if I got a medal they ought to be given out by the bucketful', I said to him. 'Because I never did anything. I had a job, though I'll admit I did it well. I really did look after my post office. I wouldn't do like some others, shut up and nip into Smithton. I wouldn't do that. I gave them every ounce.'

I suppose I did a fair bit for the people. I was very good friends with most. Sometimes I'd get a bit savage. Not very often. They'd come at all hours of the night and get their mail, and they wouldn't care. But after I got a new hip they'd ring the bell at the post office and they'd think I wasn't going to answer, it took me that long to get there. I had to walk the length of the kitchen from my bedroom to get to the post office. Everybody was telling me what I couldn't do. That got me cross. I knew what I could do. It was me that had to make up my mind what I could do. It was nearly two years before I gave up altogether.

Heather
She'd never turn anybody away. Ask a busy person and you'll get it done. That was Mum.

Ruby Paul and her daughters, c. mid 1980s. L–R: Heather Reid, Madge Breheney, Lilian Grecian, Ruby Paul, Merle Duckett

Afterword

I last saw Ruby Paul in Smithton Hospital in December 1987, ten days before her ninety-fourth birthday and three weeks before she died. She was sitting up in bed, fully alert in mind and spirit though frail in body. At my request she sang again the Boer War song of her childhood, The baby's name was *Kitchener, Gatacre, Matthew Clarendon White / Cronje Kruger, Paul Majuba, Gatacre, Warika, Lance / Kruger, Capetown, Mafeking French, Kimberley, Ladysmith, Bobs / The Union Jack, Fighting Mack, Ledite, Pretoria, Bobs*. And as she sang, with great verve and alacrity, not missing a word, she jigged up and down in bed to the tune. When I slipped back a little later for a farewell alone, she was quietly absorbed in her well-worn Bible.

At her funeral, St Stephen's Anglican church at Smithton was packed, the crowd overflowing onto the footpath. And afterwards at Merle's lovely home at Nabageena, looking out through trees across the area Ruby had loved and served for over seventy years, every cream cake and culinary confection created by loving well-wishers in Ruby's honour was worthy of a prize at the Trowutta Show.

Ruby Alice Paul was buried in the little lawn cemetery between Smithton and Stanley. The Imperial Service Medal she was awarded for her services to the community remains in the proud possession of her daughter Heather.

CM

Christobel Mattingley

Award-winning author Christobel Mattingley was educated in Tasmania at The Friends' School and graduated from the University of Tasmania in 1951. She married a Tasmanian and frequently returns from her home in South Australia to research and enjoy the island state. *Ruby of Trowutta* is her 44th book.

She has had 41 children's books published, many of which have been shortlisted, some translated, some made into films. Several are set in Tasmania. She has also written short stories, poetry, articles and film scripts. Her two earlier major works of non-fiction are the ground-breaking Aboriginal history *Survival in Our Own Land: "Aboriginal" Experiences in "South Australia" since 1836* and the widely acclaimed biography of legendary Tasmanian bushman Deny King, *King of the Wilderness*.

For her services to literature and social justice she was presented with an Advance Australia Award in 1990. In 1995 she was made a Doctor of the University of South Australia, and in 1996 a Member of the Order of Australia (AM). She received the Pheme Tanner Award from Latrobe University at Bendigo in 1999. In 1987 the City of South Perth inaugurated a Young Writers Award named in her honour.